Case History of a Film Score:

"The Thorn Birds"

By

Henry Mancini

Edited By

Roy Phillippe

Case History of a Film Score: "The Thorn Birds"

ISBN: 0-7579-2266-X

© 2004 Northridge Music Company
Sole Selling Agent: Warner Bros. Publications
Music from THE THORN BIRDS by Henry Mancini
© 1983 WB MUSIC CORP.
All Rights Reserved

By Henry Mancini
Edited by Roy Phillippe
Engraving and Layout: sinclairmusic
Project Manager: James Grupenhoff
Production Coordinator: Maudlyn Cooley
Cover Design Artist: Robert Ramsay
Special thanks to Keith Zajic and Danny Gould, WB Music, Los Angeles

TABLE OF CONTENTS

Ginny Mancini

One of the most gratifying musical experiences of my husband's career was writing the score for *The Thorn Birds*. His music was a perfect marriage with the emotional and visual ranges depicted throughout the saga of the Cleary family, and the bitter sweet love affair between Meggie and their parish priest, Ralph De Bricassart.

Meggie's Theme will live with me forever, along with the many other haunting Mancini melodies that have plucked at my heartstrings through the years.

Ginny Mancini

EDITOR'S NOTE

Henry Mancini wore many hats during his long and varied career. As a recording artist, his albums sold in the millions, he conducted every major symphony orchestra in the world, and many of his songs have become standards. He also hosted his own television series "The Mancini Generation" and authored two books, "Sounds and Scores," an orchestration text, and his autobiography "Did They Mention the Music?" However, Henry Mancini was first and foremost a composer of film music.

In 1985, Henry told me about a book he had been asked to write on the subject of film scoring using his score for the television mini–series "The Thorn Birds" as examples. Henry was excited about the project and thought the book would be unique in that it would focus on a single film's score rather than offer a broad overview of the subject. However, after submitting his manuscript, the publisher informed him that they were withdrawing their offer and were no longer interested in publishing his book.

I never forgot about Henry's book and his passion for it. I approached Warner Bros. Music Publications with the idea of putting the finishing touches on Henry's book and preparing it for publication. Since "The Thorn Birds" was a Warner Bros. production, they thought it was a good idea and told me to find out what would have to be done to complete it.

My first call was to Ginny Mancini, Henry's widow. I explained what I wanted to do and she agreed that Henry's book should be made available to music and film students and would cooperate in any way she could. Shortly thereafter I met with her assistants Jennifer Taylor Scott and Juan Attwell. With their help I was able to locate 16 music examples and 11 corresponding timing sheets. Since the timing sheets go hand in hand with the music examples, it was decided to recreate them. I was fortunate to find Celia Weiner a music editor who had worked with Henry on previous films. She had an insight as to how Henry would have wanted them written and did a wonderful job. The recreated timing sheets are for Examples 1, 4, 5, 15 and 16.

In order to check for any changes in the music that may have been made in orchestration or recording, I needed to compare Henry's sketches to the orchestrated scores as well as watch the film while reading the scores. Danny Gould at the Warner Bros. music library was able to provide the orchestrated scores from the Warner Bros. archive housed at the University of Southern California. Using Henry's sketches and the scores I was able to "resketch," so to speak, the music examples contained herein.

The accompanying compact disc contains recordings of the examples taken directly from the film soundtrack with Henry conducting.

Being a long–time fan of Henry's music made working on the book a true labor of love. Again, I thank Ginny Mancini for the privilege of being a part of bringing Henry's book to fruition.

In addition to the aforementioned, I would like to thank the following people for their assistance in making this book possible: Joseph Billé, Mike Clinco, Lisa Edmondson, Larry Kartiganer, Jon Kurnick, Laura Sharp, Sue Sinclair, and Terry Woodson. A special thank you goes to my wife, Linda, for her love and encouragement.

Roy Phillippe
July 2003

Roy Phillippe and Henry Mancini at the American Society of Music Arrangers Award Dinner on May 25, 1993 at the Century Plaza Hotel, Los Angeles, California

Part I
Pre-Production

PREFACE

First came the call. The call was to my agent, Al Bart, from producer Stan Margulies asking about my availability to compose the score for a mini--series he was doing called "The Thorn Birds." The nine-hour (later expanded to ten) series was to be aired on the ABC television network the following spring (1983) and was to be presented by David Wolper and Stan Margulies. I had previously worked with Stan and David in 1972 on the theatrical film, "Visions of Eight," a unique movie about the Munich Olympics.

The next call was from Al to me. The only thing I recall saying is, "When do I start?" The book by Colleen McCullough was, of course, a number one best seller world wide. The lovers, Father Ralph de Bricassart (Richard Chamberlain) and Meggie Cleary (Rachel Ward), were known to millions. Drogheda ranked with Tara as the best-known homestead in modern fiction. With Australia as the setting, the epic-sized story was indeed awesome. The depth of the public's interest was demonstrated when the show aired on ABC on March 27, 28, 29 and 30, 1983. More people watched "The Thorn Birds" than had watched any mini-series to that date.

My contract was negotiated with Dick Harris, head of the music department at Warner Bros. Studios, where the film was being produced.

The first order of business was to read the book. Next, I was sent the script. I should say I was sent four scripts. Each one was about the size of a standard theatrical film script. They were the work of writer, Carmen Culver. As I read I was elated to find that she had indeed captured the essence of the novel, not an easy task considering the complexity and size of the story.

Also, as I read, I realized that I was into a project that would call upon all my movie scoring experience which had started at Universal Studios in 1952. Many of the the problems a film composer encounters were present. Not the least of these was the amount of music to be written. The final total was four hours, give or take a minute or two. EPICS must be served!

This book is a step by step account of my work on "The Thorn Birds." It deals with the real problems and the real people one encounters in this profession.

PRE-PRODUCTION

It was April, 1982, and the shooting was scheduled to begin on June 1. The script called for a large amount of on-camera music, music that had to be sung, played or danced to by the actors. The style and/or tempo of this muic had to be decided upon. For this purpose a meeting was called, one of several that we had on the same subject. Present were producer Margulies, director Daryl Duke, Danny Gould, liason for Warner Bros. music department, and me.

Every major studio music department has a person whose job it is to read the scripts, sometimes long before a composer is assigned, and to spot any references to music indicated by the writer. If an established copyright is needed he will "clear" the music. This means that he will contact the Harry Fox Agency, which is the central agency used by all of the studios for music clearance, or he will contact the publisher directly. He will tell them what the piece is and how it is being used in the film. They, in turn, will come back with a "quote," or fee, which must be paid by the producer if that music is used. Ninety-nine percent of the music in "The Thorn Birds" was either original or in the public domain.

Danny Gould had compiled a complete list of all the music that had to be prepared before shooting commenced. Music of this type falls under the general heading of what we call "source music," music coming from a visual source, be it human or mechanical (i. e. a television set, record player, juke box, etc.). Using Danny's list as a guide, we set out to find the proper music for each spot.

In Episodes One and Two there were scenes that called for Fiona Cleary (Jean Simmons) to be playing the piano. Classical pieces were indicated. The character was able to play fairly well. In both cases she was playing the piano to vent some of the pain that she was going through. Therefore, the music had to reflect a certain sadness and underlying anger toward the lot she had been dealt in life. After much discussion and listening to recordings, we decided upon a Chopin Nocturne Op. 62 No. 2 and for the second piece, Ballade Op. 10 No. 1 by Brahms. It was a fortunate break for us that Miss Simmons actually was able to play the piano. She was sent the recordings and music of the pieces and was informed as to which sections she would be miming.

In such cases commercial recordings, if suitable, are used. The terms "temp tracks" or "guide tracks" are employed for this processs. Of course, we had to replace those recordings after the scenes were shot. Miss Simmons did a very creditable job of miming on screen, thus making my job much easier. Every film composer at one time or another has had close encounters of the worst kind trying to replace temp tracks. We are often called on to replace tracks of an entire ensemble of musicians playing on camera. These players are referred to as side-line musicians. Wind players must phrase and breathe in sync with the their fellow players on the screen. String players must match bowings. Rhythm players have their problems also. It would be a bit disconcerting to have the drummer on screen playing a ride cymbal while we hear him playing the snare drum on the final track. Of course, it's up to the composer to see that everything he writes matches the on-screen players. Whenever possible we try to pre-record the actual music that will remain in the finished film. The on-screen musicians are then in perfect sync with the music, thus eliminating the hairy problem of replacement of the track later.

After the scene was shot, the seemingly simple task of replacing Miss Simmons' track took some careful preparation. You might think that a pianist could simply look at the screen and play along in perfect sync. Think again.

Enter now the composer's best friend and confidant, the music editor, also referred to as the music cutter. Strangely, he neither edits nor cuts. What he does do has always seemed to me to be the greatest of all magic acts. His various functions will be referred to throughout this book. On "The Thorn Birds" my man was Jay Smith.

For these scenes his job was to provide a guide track for the pianist who would come in to replace the temp tracks. Two devices could be employed, the click track and the streamer. The first involves the ear, the second involves the eye. One or both of these devices are used according to what is needed to help the pianist. There are two types of click tracks. The first is produced by punching a hole about the size of a safety match head in the center of a strip of 35 mm. blank film. When this hole passes over the sound head of the projector, a sharp "click" sound is produced. The second is produced by the electronic digital metronome. This is useful when the tempo remains constant throughout an entire piece. Since both Chopin and Brahms were not concerned with our problems, the digital click was of no use here.

All of the music editor's work is done on a black and white dupe (copy) of the film. This holds true for the sound effects and dialogue people. Any change in the color (master) print must be applied to the dupes to avoid chaos later on.

Jay set about building a variable click track, one that would match each nuance of the original piano recording. This is done on a moviola, which is actually a machine that has a small viewing screen. The film, on 1,000-foot reels, is run through the viewer controlled by a foot pedal. The film can be run at regular speed, slow or fast speeds and also can be run backward and forward at will.

The scene with the temp track was run on the viewing screen, and the blank film was run, in sync, on another sound head on the same machine. He then proceeded to follow the temp track and punch the clicks in perfect sync with it on the blank film. The pianist would, of course, hear the clicks through earphones.

The player is also helped visually by means of a streamer. This is a vertical white line that crosses the screen from left to right. When the line hits the right end of the screen that is your sync point right on the button. The line is made by the music editor. He uses a straight-edged scriber that scrapes the emulsion from the film, thus creating the white line. Jay and I looked at the scene to see where these lines should be placed to be of the greatest help to our pianist. With these aids in place, we were ready to record. With one eye on the music, we were ready to record. With one eye on the music, the other on the screen, and both ears listening to the clicks (and the temp track if necessary), the recording went off without a hitch. Fiona Cleary never sounded better.

Next on the list was music for Mary Carson's (Barbara Stanwyck) grand birthday party. Several factors had to be considered. The period, which was 1920. The kind of dance music that would be played then. The make-up of the orchestra that would play the music. After some discussion I suggested a seven-piece band consisting of fiddle, cornet, accordion, banjo, upright piano, tuba and drums. Director Daryl Duke figured that for this purpose he needed a waltz, a fox trot, a jazzy up-beat number and finally a "Black Bottom" dance piece. Since we had no idea how long each piece would last, we decided to use temp tracks. Danny had assembled some music for us to listen to, from which four pieces were selected. These four recordings were used on the set for the shooting of the scene. The side-line musicians followed along as the records, now transferred to tape, were played. Later we would replace the recordings in the same manner described above in the piano scenes.

The opening of Episode Two involved Father Ralph's arrival at his new assignment in Sydney. As he entered the church there was a group of choir boys singing in the loft. They were accompanied by an organ. The piece indicated in the script was Casar Franck's "Panis Angelicus." Since the piece was in the public domain world wide, it was not necessary to clear it. The sequence ran three minutes and fifteen seconds. Opening credits were run during the scene. We decided to make a guide track using an organ and three soprano singers. The choir boys on camera mimed to this track. We used the digital metronome for tempo so that we would have the proper tempo when we dropped the temp tracks and added a new organ track and a new boys choir track later.

Later in the show there was a scene in which the new hired hands drive into Drogheda on horse–drawn hay wagons. Among the workers was Luke O'Neill (Bryan Brown) who later married Meggie. The script called for the men to be singing as they drove in. An Australian folk song was in order. We settled on the well–known "Botany Bay." I felt that it would be effective to have a solo singer playing guitar on the verses with other men joining in on the chorus. This track had to be permanent because the men were to be photographed singing. Our guitarist, soloist and eight–man chorus made the track that was heard in the film.

After their wool–shearing chores are finished a few months later, they leave, again on the wagons and again singing. The same procedure was followed, except this time the tune was "Old Bullock Dray." Luke remained. He and Meggie were destined to get together.

On their first date, a workers' dance at a nearby woolshed, we needed more dance music. This dance was hardly as grand as Mary Carson's party. Just three not–quite–ready–for–prime–time musicians were used. Fiddle, accordion and guitar. Temp tracks were used and later replaced.

In Episode Three Luke and Meggie were married, and they moved north to Queensland to start their new life together. Later, Luke and his mate, Arnie, showed up decked out in kilts to take Meggie to a Scottish dance. Of course, we needed bagpipes. Danny once again supplied us with several recordings to choose from. We picked a lively number to shoot the scene to and, of course, replaced it with a real live bagpiper later.

Later during a communion scene it was indicated that a choir would be singing "The Lord's Prayer." I checked with Father Terrence Sweeney, a Jesuit, and our religious advisor on the picture. He told me that in the well–known popular version the final words are: "For Thine is the Kingdom, etc." This was the Protestant version. the Roman Cathoolic version, which we needed here, ends just before those words with: "But deliver us from evil, Amen." I wrote a new Roman Catholic version. This was replaced by a ten–piece, mixed–voice choir. A temp track was made.

All of the tracks were prepared on quarter–inch tape and then turned over to the sound man on the shooting stage. This completed the pre–production phase. Director Duke had all of the musical material he would need for the next five months. The picture commenced shooting June 1, 1982 and ended on October 27, 1982.

THE THEMES

With the pre-production phase completed, the next move was to assemble my original thematic material, which would be the backbone of the score. Since I prefer not to watch dailies (the screening of all un-cut film shot on the previous day), my next contact with the film would be viewing the first rough cut many weeks later. This provided ample time for me to work out my themes. It also gave me a chance to soak up some atmosphere on the elaborate set that had been built in the Simi Valley just north of the San Fernando Valley. The set was a marvel. The barren land was transformed into Drogheda, complete with the main house, the Cleary's home, the wool shed, a large paddock, the borehead, a cemetery and more than enough sheep to create the illusion of the Australian locale. It was a beautiful set, and, one that was destined to be torn down once the filming was finished.

By this time I was thoroughly familiar with the story and the characters. Two main themes were emerging. One was Drogheda itself and the other was the Father Ralph and Meggie love story. I titled the first "The Thorn Birds Theme" and the other "Meggie's Theme."

I had quite a wrestling match with "The Thorn Birds Theme." I wrote and rejected at least three pieces before I settled on the one that was used. My research of Australian music, most of which was done by means of ethnic recordings, turned up the fact that the music was simple and direct. In the songs the words were of a story-telling sort and very honest. I guess that description would apply to the folk music of most countries including America's. Musically, a strong Gallic influence was evident. Not surprising, considering that many of the early settlers came from Ireland. The instruments used were the guitar, banjo, fiddle, accordion, mandolin, harmonica, bass and, in some cases, drums. In listening to one particular recording a strange sound caught my attention. Its droning sound was unsophisticated and earthy. It complimented perfectly the visual image of a vast land and of simple people. It was a DULCIMER, a member of the guitar family dating back a few centuries. I had the sound. Now I needed the music.

First I needed to find someone who could play it well and also demonstrate what the instrument could or couldn't do. After many inquiries I found a fine session guitarist, Jon Kurnick. He came over, dulcimer in hand, and gave me a thorough demonstration. In addition to having two tunable drone strings, there were two melody strings tuned in unison. The frets were spaced modally. Chromatic passages were not possible. The range was roughly a tenth, from middle "C" to the "E" above. With these limitations in mind, the opening strain of the theme took shape. I wrote the opening strain that featured the dulcimer and had Jon come in and record it on a small tape cassette. This I played for Stan Margulies who agreed that it sounded perfect for the locale. In fact, all of the main themes were demonstrated in this manner.

Knowing in advance that this theme would be getting a great deal of exposure, I felt that it must contain several varying sections in order to avoid the pitfall of "here comes that theme again." The opening credits of the first episode alone were over five minutes, quite a long time to sustain interest. The form ended up being: A – B – C – B – A – plus and extension.

Example 1
The Thorn Birds Theme

"Meggie's Theme" was quite another thing. It was the main "love theme." Here again there were several rejects. I finally settled on a "timeless," classical approach. The piece would be quite evident throughout the film. Therefore, its "tensile" strength had to hold up. The proper theme is of prime importance. It should lend itself to a wide variety of interpolation and orchestration. The opening phrase is a prime concern. Many times just a hint of the melody is very effective and helpful to the score.

In the past, in some cases, in order to break the traditional form, I have extended the final section of a theme. Here it occurs six bars after the bridge. I went up to a kind of "surge" that gives the theme a peak, very useful in the more dramatic situations.

Example 2
Meggie's Theme

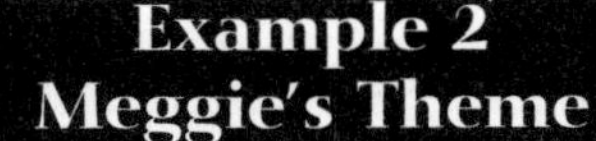

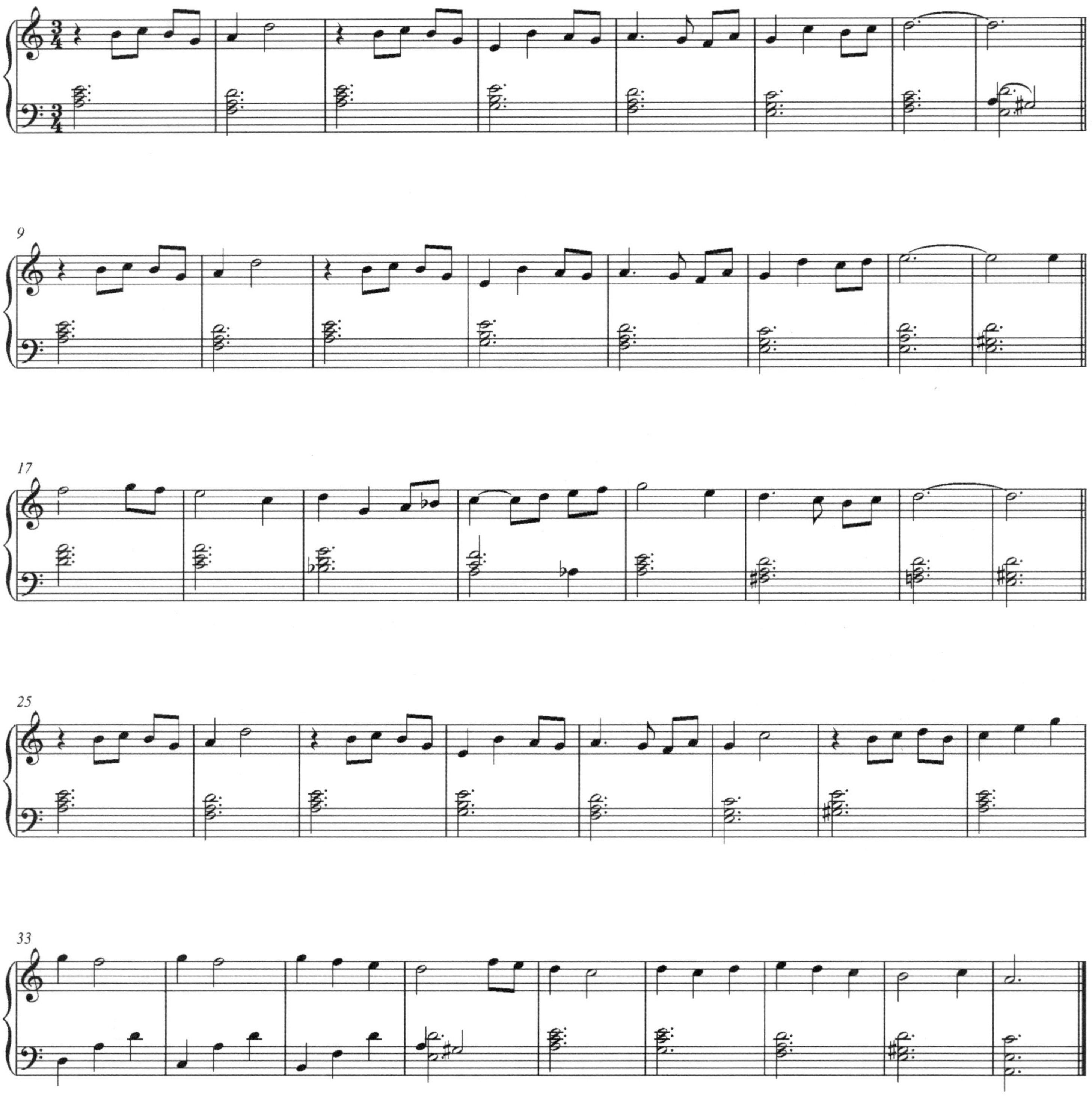

Mary Carson, the Grande Dame of Drogheda, was the catalyst who set into motion the many twists and turns in the story. She appeared in the first episode only. Having been rejected in her romantic advances toward Ralph de Bricassart, she set out, through her last will, on a devious scheme that affects profoundly the lives of Meggie and Ralph. Her character had a great undercurrent of frustration and revenge. Her theme has a brooding quality dramatically opposite to diatonic approach of "Meggie's Theme." The mood is darkly enhanced by the changing chromatic harmonies.

Example 3
The Mary Carson Theme

Though only a few in number, the scenes between Paddy (Richard Kiley) and Fiona Cleary were quite touching. Paddy was a simple man of the soil who wasn't capable of a single evil thought. Although Fi had every reason to resent her situation, her attitude toward Paddy was always one of love and respect. He revered her. I felt that a simple folk–like theme would properly underscore this relationship. I wrote an Irish tune that harked back to the land that Paddy had left years before.

Example 4
The Paddy and Fi Theme

The relationship between Luke O'Neill and Meggie indicated a secondary love theme. Wheras "Meggie's Theme" was in a minor key, the "Luke and Meggie Theme" was in a major key. This was to help establish a feeling of hope and promise for their future. Meggie really felt that she could overcome the frustation and hopelessness that her love for Ralph had given her. Major key notwithstanding, her marriage to Luke soon ended.

Example 5
The Luke and Meggie Theme

Over the years, in many films, I have encountered scenes that do not have, and should not have any relationship to the thematic material in the rest of the picture. I think of these as "set pieces." I look forward to these as they offer a relief from the sometimes oft–repeated main themes. "The Thorn Birds" offered several: Ralph's elated arrival at the Vatican, Meggie's lonely arrival at the idyllic retreat, Matlock Island, and the sheep–shearing contest between Luke and Bob Cleary. Some examples of these, in part, will be shown later.

A final word on the subject of themes. "The Thorn Birds" was a film, that, because of its scope and sweep, dictated the use of melodic underscoring. Many pictures, however, would be sunk in the water if this approach were used. Some great scores have used orchestral and/or elec–tronic sounds and textures to great effect throughout the entire film without an identifiable melody in sight. Atonal or serial music has been favored by many. The approach to the music to be written for any given film is a subject that must be given careful thought by the composer. It is then imperative to communicate to your employer, by any means necessary, what you intend to do. Don't forget that it's his film, and he has the final word on which music stays in the picture. One flick of the finger in the final dubbing stage can reduce several days' work to silence.

My former boss at Universal, Joe Gershenson, used to say, "Take partners!" This sage advice, if taken will eliminate many hassles on the recording stage.

SPOTTING THE FILM

My first viewing of the rough cut of Episode One was on September 13. Stan Margulies, David Wolper, director Daryl Duke, writer Carmen Culver, plus several production people were present. The film was far from finalized, but it helped me a great deal to find out what was in store for me. After the screening, the group exchanged comments on what was lacking and how it could be remedied. If the subject of music brought up I voiced my feelings. If not, I was strictly an observer. These sessions can get to be quite frank. Unless I am on firm ground, my lips are sealed.

Stan said that much work had to be done before I could begin work. It is useless and foolhardy to start detailed writing before the print is absolutely finalized. I saw it again the following week. It was vastly improved, but it still needed work. With more fine-tuning the film was ready. However, one big hurdel remained: the ABC network's final approval. Their answer was an enthusiastic go-ahead. In fact, the network was not a problem in any of the four episodes.

October 7 was set as the spotting day. Since director Duke was still shooting the film, Stan was at the helm. He and I were to spend many, many hours together both in the projection room and on the scoring stage in the months to come.

Joining us for the spotting was music editor, Jay Smith. His job was to write, in longhand, the exact starts and stops of the music sequence (cues) that we decided upon. Any comments pertinent to the musical treatment of any given scene was noted. He was also at the controls when we wanted to back the film up and look at a scene again. One of the several film editors, Bob Shugrue, was also with us. He was there to observe what we were doing so that later, if any changes were made in the film, he could better relate to Jay regarding their effects on the music.

There were several scenes that were being shot or re-shot and added to the picture later. He told us where these would be placed. This situation is less than ideal. However, time was starting to become a factor, so we had to go ahead and worry about the additions later. "Absolutely finalized" was now "nearly finalized."

Episodes One and Four were three-hour films. Episodes Two and Three were two hours long. Because of commercials, station breaks, promos, etc., the actual running time of a three-hour segment is about two hours and twenty-three minutes. A two-hour segment runs about one hour and thirty-five minutes.

Normally the black and white work-print we use is set up on 1,000 foot reels. The cue numbers are designated according to the reel that they are in, i. e., Reel One - the cues would be 1-M-1, 1-M-2, 1-M-3, etc. In reel two they would be 2-M-1, 2-M-2, 2-M-3, etc. We knew that adding scenes later would throw the reels off balance. A cue that was at the end of reel five could end up in reel six. Therefore, we decided that the M-(music) numbers would run consecutively from M-1 through the final number in the episode. Any additions would simply be assigned an "X" number, M-2X if it followed M-2. In the first episode we went up to M-44. The total number of music cues for the entire picture was 131.

The proper placement of music in a film is secondary only to the music itself. We ran each reel, stopping very often to discuss whether or not the scene in question really needed music, and, if so, what kind, and when it should start and stop. The dramatic and romantic nature of "The Thorn Birds" story had a built-in trap; the over-use of music. We had to take great care to avoid the wall-to-wall music syndrome. Silence can be the composer's best friend.

The number down the right-hand side indicated to Jay the reel number plus the film footage at the start of each cue. As I finish each piece I will circle the M-number indicating the completion. On the far left side of the page I will write down the instruments used. This provides a quick reference when I start to schedule the recording sessions.

Overall, the spotting took about six hours. Jay's first order of business then was to type up the notes he had made. These handwritten notes are more often turned over to a stenographer for typing. They are referred to, naturally enough, as "Music Spotting Notes," not to be confused with the "Detailed Music Timings" that he would do soon after. The music spotting notes are very important. In the following example you can see exactly what information is given: the exact length, a brief description of the scene and the precise starting and stopping points. This enables me to start my planning of the size and make-up of the orchestra and the amount of time I'll need to record.

The number down the right-hand side indicates to Jay the reel number plus the film footage at the start of each cue. As I finish each piece I will circle the M-number indicating its completion. On the far left side of the page I will write down the instruments used. This provides a quick reference when I start to schedule the recording sessions.

Example 6

THE THORN BIRDS #167601
Episode One

MUSIC SPOTTING NOTES

M-1 (4:13.3) — MAIN TITLE starts at the beginning of the show, covering Ralph's long drive in; under Mrs. Smith's greetings as he enters the house. Out as they close the door behind them. — 15+2 R-1

M-2 (1:09.5) — After Mary's opening dialogue with Ralph, music starts on cut to Pete as he signals the start of the race between Ralph and one of the ranch hands; under the race and ends after Mary congratulates Ralph and tells him the horse is his. Out as Ralph says: "AND I'LL TAKE GREAT PLEASURE IN RIDING HIM WHENEVER I'M HERE, BUT..." — 667+10 R-1

M-3 (:18.4) — After the race, Mary mentions that someday she'll have to give Drogheda to somebody. Mary: "THAT'S WORTH THINKING ABOUT" and rides off. Music starts as Ralph looks after her. Ends in time lapse as he looks at Mary's portrait up to his dialogue with Mrs. Smith. — 941+1 R-1

M-4 (:59.4) — PIANO SOURCE at the church of the marching children in the yard. Ends in cut to new scene. — 257+1 R-2

M-5 (1:53.3) — Ralph has gone to the station to meet Paddy and his family, which he meets one by one. Then Meggy appears from in back of her brothers. Music starts as she stops, looking up at Ralph; under their arrival at Drogheda and dial. with Mary to Act Out. — 429+15 R-2

M-6 (1:46.6) — ACT In as we see the sheep being herded in. Alternate ending as Mary first speaks to Paddy at :34.0. Music ends after diss. to Meggy entering Paddy's house and out as Fiona speaks to her. — 610+1 R-2

M-7 (1:27.1) — Mary and Fiona have been having a serious conversation about why Fiona married Paddy. Music starts on cut to Meggie approaching the wool shed. Under her fascination with the place. Music ends on cut to Frank feeding the barking dogs. — 12+2 R-3

THE THORN BIRDS #167601

Music Spotting Notes (Con't)

M-8 (:43.5)	Paddy and Frank have been having an argument and Frank offers to fight him, but Paddy doesn't want that. Music starts after Paddy says: "NOW GET BACK TO WORK!" a good beat after the cut to Fiona watching. They go their separate ways as Fiona goes back into the house. Then Ralph arrives in his car. Out dial. Ralph and Fiona.	580+4 R-3
M-9 (2:21.7)	Ralph watches Meggie as Meggie watches her brothers ride off and she looks after them wistfully. Must starts as she starts to bend down to scratch in the dirt with a stick, while Fiona and Ralph discuss her. Meggie shows Ralph her wool barn, but Mary enters to darken the scene. SEGUE to M-10	784+ R-3
M-10 (1:28.7)	SEGUE from M-9 on cut to the kangaroos hopping across the pastureland. We see Pete mending fences with Stu, under their dial. Thru the diss. to Meggie's brothers drinking from their canteen. Out their dial.	210+9 R-4
M-11 (1:25.3)	Pete is talking to the boys, telling them not to waste their water, when the dog starts barking and they turn to see what's the matter. Music starts on cut to the wild boar, and Stuie aiming his rifle at the boar as it charges him, to Act Out.	379+5 R-4
M-12 (2:43.3)	Paddy is standing on the porch talking to Stuie about something that happened between him and his father. Music starts after Paddy says: "HE NEVER CALLED ME A COWARD AGAIN AFTER THAT," and as Stuie looks over at him, and they smile at each other. Under dinner table scene. Under dial. of Paddy and Fiona in their bedroom (tenderness) and ends on CUT to Pete singing.	913+1 R-4
M-13	Production track: Pete singing (as is.)	
M-14 (1:18.8)	While Pete demonstrates the correct way to shear a sheep, one of the boys does his own job. Pete says: "I'D SAY YOU'RE A CHAMPION SHEARER...IN THE MAKING." Music starts after the sheep's baaa. We cut to the big sheep drive. Music ends on Ralph praying under a tree.	423+1 R

THE THORN BIRDS #167601

Music Spotting Notes (Con't)

M-15 (1:20.6)	SOURCE: Fiona playing the piano (we will redo it with more fire.)	12+2 R-6
M-16 (2:46.4)	Ralph gets soaked in the rain and runs up onto the front porch to get out of his wet clothes. He takes all his clothes off and begins drying himself with the towel, as camera pans over to a window. Music starts as camera holds on Mary watching him; under their dial; Ralph prays in the chapel; Out on cut to Meggie at the sump.	472+12 R-6
M-17 (:36.6)	At the sump, Frank is talking to Meggie. He lifts her up bythe shoulders and says: "NOW LISTEN TO ME..." Music starts here and continues under their dialogue to~~that One~~.	814+8 R-6

"THE THORN BIRDS" #167601

Music Spotting Notes (Con't)

M-18
(5:45)

SOURCE: Music for the Fair. Music starts at
the beginning of the act. Ends on CUT to the
interior fighting ring.

21+0
R-7

M-19
(1:11.3)

Frank and Meggie have been talking and he's been
trying to explain to her why he's leaving. With
tears in her eyes, she asks: "I WISH YOU'D TAKE ME
WITH YOU, WILL YOU, FRANK?" Music starts as he
starts to stand up. Then he walks away and she
stands sobbing. Out on CUT to Paddy talking
(music must be out by then.)

543+1
R-8

M-20
(1:15.4)

Paddy has been talking to Ralph, telling him just
how he happened to marry Fiona, that her family
was willing to pay him to take her away. Music
starts a good beat after Paddy says: "SHE WAS
SO BEAUTIFUL!" Music ends on CUT to Father Ralph
climbing the stairs to Meggie's bedroom.

733+15
R-8

M-21
(2:43.9)

After his talk with Paddy, Ralph returns to the
rectory and climbs the stairs to Meggie's
bedroom. The housekeeper tells him she's
finally fallen asleep. Ralph walks in to her
bedside. Music starts a beat after he stops,
looking down at her. Ends in the Act Out.

55+3
R-9

M-22
(1:32.0)

Play in from commercial. (A new scene will be
shot to precede what's here now) It now starts
with Ralph just having dropped Meggie off from
school and he takes off again. Out under dial.
between Meggie and Fiona.

311+2
R-9

M-23
(1:10.3)

Ralph has just paid an angry visit to Mary to
find out why she took Meggie out of school,
but Mary believes that Ralph's interest in the
girl is more than spiritual. Music starts on
the cut to Fiona brushing her hair in her bedroom
(night). She reads Frank's newspaper clipping
while Paddy pretends to be asleep. SEGUE to
M-24 in diss. to a day shot of Ralph and Meggie
riding.

12+2
R-10

"THE THORN BIRDS" #167601

Music Spotting Notes (Con't)

M-24
(129.8)

SEGUE from M-23 in dissolve to a day shot of Ralph 117+8
and Meggie riding. This is a montage of several   R-10
shots of them enjoying each other's company. Diss.
to Ralph and Meggie entering the house, under
their dial. and ends under Mary's dial. as she
descends the stairs.

M-25
(2:30.5)

Paddy arrives home to find that the new baby is 591+0
seriously ill. While they're waiting for the   R-10
doctor to arrive, the time is spent in prayer.
Then the wheezing sounds from the baby stop.
Music starts as Paddy lifts his head to look
over at the dead baby. SEGUE to M-26 on CUT
to 6-month time-lapse shot of Ralph driving
toward Drogheda.

M-26
(1:01.8)

SEGUE from M-25 in time-lapse shot of Ralph 816+11
arriving at Drogheda. We cut to Meggie coming   R-10/11
out of the outhouse and feeling sick. Stu
tells Ralph that something very strange is
happening with her. Music ends on cut to Meggie
in the wool barn.

M-27
(2:02.8)

Meggie finally confesses her awful secret to 239+5
Ralph, that she's dying of some dreaded disease.   R-11
Ralph finally realizes what it is and says to
her: "MY PRECIOUS GIRL, YOU'RE NOT DYING. YOU'RE
GROWING UP!" Music starts after this line and
continues under their dialogue in the rose garden,
and ends in the Act Out.

M-28
(1:18.1)

SOURCE: Orchestra tune-up only, after Mrs. Smith 645+10
tells Fiona that she looks stunning. Tune-up   R-11
ends on CUT to the buffet table. SEGUES with M-29.

M-29
(1:24.3)

RECITAL SOURCE MUSIC SEGUES from M-28 on CUT to 762+13
the buffet table. Recital music ends as the   R-11
maid with the canapes leaves Ralph.

M-30
(1:32.5)

Several of the party guests are talking when one 20+7
of them looks up and asks who the girl is. Music R-12
starts on CUT of Meggie coming down the stairs.
Music ends on CUT to Mary as Paddy introduces her.

"THE THORN BIRDS" #167601

Music Spotting Notes (Con't)

M-31
(3:57.0)
SOURCE: Waltz music after Ralph asks Mary to dance, starting four bars before they begin to dance. Music ends just after last cut of Paddy and Fiona dancing before Meggie approaches Ralph.
291+6
R-12

M-32
(1:45.3)
SOURCE: New ballad starts about 10 seconds after M-31 ends. Continues under dialogue to Act Out. (No visual dancing on this one).
663+8
R-12

M-33
(1:08.3)
SOURCE: New flapper-type dance on the plan-in from commercial. Ends in Meggie's cut of being downcast as the woman walks away from her toward Ralph.
21+1
R-13

M-34
(1:15.2)
SOURCE: "The Black Bottom" as Ralph starts to dance with the woman. Ends after Ralph walks out of the ballroom and we don't see the dancers anymore.
148+11
R-13

M-35
(1:17.1)
After Ralph walks Mary upstairs, she admits to him that she has always loved him. Mary: "SO MUCH SO I WOULD HAVE KILLED YOU FOR NOT WANTING ME!" and cut to Ralph, and Music starts on CUT back to Mary. Muusic ends after she closes the doors, about 1/2 second before CUT to Ralph coming down the stairs.
423+9
R-13

M-36
(:40.9)
SOURCE: The orchestra plays "Good Night, Ladies," which is P.D. and is right for the period. Music ends on cut to Meggie riding the horse.
543+14
R-13

M-37
(:49.2)
Ralph tells Meggie that she must not think of him in any romantic way and that someday she will meet the man she's supposed to marry. He helps her off her horse. Music starts on the cut to Ralph and Meggie walking. Ends in Act Out.
823+3
R-13

M-38
(1:16.0)
Mary has died, and Mrs. Smith tells Ralph, who hurries to her room. Music starts after the cut to Ralph entering the bedroom. Music ends as Ralph speaks to Mrs. Smith
59+4
R-14

<u>"THE THORN BIRDS" #167601</u>

Music Spotting Notes (Con't)

M-39 (:43.3)	Funeral music on cut to the funeral procession, as Ralph reads in Latin. Thru the diss. and out as Ralph starts to give the eulogy.	603+5 R-14
M-40 (1:49.2)	In the final scene, Ralph is talking to Meggie. She begs him: "YOU CAN MARRY ME. YOU LOVE ME!" Ralph says: "BUT I LOVE GOD MORE!" Music starts after his line as he takes his hand away from her chin. Music ends in the final Act Out.	604+11 R-15
M-41 (:39.3)	END CREDITS	778+9 R-14
BUMPER #1 (:05.3)		
BUMPER #2 (:07.3)		

Modern technology now steps in with a helping hand. A video-cassette of the film is made and given to me, making it unnecessary to leave my work studio at home while I am writing. Some of my colleagues find it more comfortable to work with a moviola. However, all of us have worked from only the timing sheets, if necessary.

I think an outline of my work process would be in order at this point.

In most cases I prefer to work in sequence, i. e., from the beginning to the end. In many cases, I have put the Main Title aside. Usually, the correct length of the titles is not finalized until quite near to the recording dates. However, with "The Thorn Birds" the titles were nailed down from the very beginning.

I will view a scene from my cassette several times in order to get its feeling and pace. I will examine it carefully noting the points along the way that will need emphasis or a change of pace. The tempo of the scene takes shape. After becoming thoroughly familiar with the film, I put the cassette aside and turn to the timing sheets. I tick off the points that I feel need attention. Working from the timing sheets I then decide what my tempo – or tempi – will be. If I opt for a click track, I will indicate it at the top of the sketch as you will see in the music examples later. If I decide on free timing I will hold the stop watch with my right hand, thus deciding in this manner the number of seconds in each bar. Before a note is written, the entire cue is timed in this method. Imagine a sketch page with no music on it, just timings, and you have the picture. With clicks, and of course, free timings, the timings are indicated at each bar line. At brisk tempos, every two bars. Arriving at the proper tempo is all-important to the success of the music. Having to slow down or speed up to reach a sync point is not acceptable for the professional film composer.

THE LOGISTICS

Logic tells us that a composer cannot wait until he has finished his score to call the orchestra. Los Angeles has a group of musicians working in the studios that is second to none anywhere. The specialists are always booked up several months in advance. Therefore, you must make up your mind about your orchestra at the time you start writing.

The period of time that occurs from the completion of principle photography until the delivery of the completed print to the network is called the POST PRODUCTION period. The music, dialogue and sound effects people must all work on a schedule dictated by that delivery date.

My spotting notes showed that there were one hour and twenty minutes of music in the first show. Considering that the average theatrical film contains from thirty to forty–five minutes of music, this was a considerable amount. The two main areas that differ between composing for television versus theatricals are time and money. Television comes up short in both.

Because of the amount of music involved I felt that I needed six three–hour sessions. I could go into overtime if I had to. The dates were set: November 30, December 1 and 2. The maximum number of minutes recorded music allowed in one three–hour session by the American Federation of Musicians is fifteen, breaking down, of course, to five minutes an hour, noting that the orchestra must have a ten–minute break every hour. Being practical, a realistic average would be three minutes an hour or maybe ten minutes over the three–hour period.

I had enough time for the first one, but as the remaining shows became available, the time between spotting and recording was shorter and shorter. At times I was writing one episode and spotting the next at the same time. The final recording session of the whole series was on March 15, 1983. We went on the air on March 27. The grand total of all the recording sessions was twenty–five.

Producer Stan Margulies was the keeper of the treasury. Therefore, the size of the orchestra was in his domain. Because of the nature of the film he knew we had to have a sound which would not undercut the considerable on–screen production values. He was generous. His only comment to me was, "Use what you need, but don't kill me." With Stan's health in mind, I set about assembling the orchestra. It broke down into several groups. The first was the full orchestra. It numbered fifty–one players.

Strings	**Brass**	**Woodwinds**	**Remaining**
12 violins	3 trumpets	2 flutes (with doubles)	1 harp/Irish harp
6 violas	3 french horns	2 clarinets/bass clarinets	2 12–string guitars
6 celli	3 trombones	1 oboe/english horn	1 dulcimer
4 basses	1 tuba	1 bassoon	1 autoharp
			1 percussion
			1 keyboard

The second group was the same, minus the three trumpets.

The third was minus the trumpets, three trombones and tuba. The three french horns remained.

The fourth was minus the three french horns, guitars, autoharp and dulcimer. Strings, woodwinds, harp, keyboard, and percussion were left.

Small groups of various numbers were used to replace the temp-tracks and also to record the atmospheric music that was needed for the Italian and Greek sections. The full orchestra was used for one session on each of the four shows.

The make-up of my string section, led by concertmaster, Erno Neufeld, was a prime concern to me, since they were involved in practically everything from start to finish. Once the brass was released I needed a string combination that would give me a full sound, especially in the low and medium registers. The six violas, six celli and four basses, although not of symphonic proportions, proved to be quite useful. The unison lines were full without the forcing one could expect from a smaller section. In divisi writing they would provide a warm underpinning for the top line. My reasoning for the twelve violins was simple: I had no use, dramatically, for a soaring top end. If I kept the unison violins mainly within the staff and the divisi to no more than four on a part, I knew that I could maintain a balanced and full-sounding section.

My woodwind section was made up basically of four soloists: Flutes – Louise Ditullio, Clarinet – Dominick Fera, Oboe/English Horn – Arnold Koblentz and Bassoon – Mike O'Donovan. Another flue and clarinet provided capabilities for various unisons and chordal writing within the section.

The ten brass players took care of business quite well, although the tutti brass had relatively little to do. The trombones and the tuba were called upon in the more dramatic scenes to add darkness and weight. The French horns were used more often with the strings and the wood-winds.

The remaining playerss were each there for a particular reason. The harpist played Irish harp throughout most of the score. The Irish harp, which is tuned diatonically is a member of the lute family, and is an ancient country cousin of today's chromatic harp. Before each piece it must be tuned to the scale required for the music. Having no pedals, it hasn't the capability of changing notes mid-stream. Its value is in its sound, which is attractively imperfect. Earthy would be another way of putting it. It was an unusual color used alone or with the strings and woods.

We spoke of dulcimer earlier.

There were scenes, many involving "The Thorn Birds Theme," that called for a rhythmic pulse. My rhythm section consisted of two twelve-string guitars. They added just the right ethnic feeling and sound I was looking for. The autoharp reinforced that feeling at times.

Our keyboard player spent most of his time playing a muted Yamaha upright piano. Being a composer who uses a piano when writing, I had been using this instrument at home for several years. It is a traditional upright with one difference; the middle pedal locks down in place, causing a ribbon of felt to come between the hammers and the strings. Those of you who have to contend with thin walls and tone-deaf neighbors might do well to check this out. It has a sound of its own, much more soft and subtle than the regular piano. It was an extremely useful color.

The percussionist, usually hidden in a maze of equipment, had an easy time in this score. His "arsenal" consisted only of timpani, vibes and song bells, a softer and more delicate version of the standard orchestra bells. Most of his time was spent on the song bells playing along with the muted piano and the Irish harp. The three of them were used frequently.

Enter now the person whose job it was to assemble the orchestra, the ORCHESTRA CON-TRACTOR. She was Patti De Caro. I had definite preferences as to which players I wanted. If some were not available, we would discuss others. Her job was to put out a work call to each and every player we needed. She also had to make sure that the people were paid properly. This can become a detailed and complicated task due to the players who double on other instruments and players receive over-scale payments. Later, if the score should be released as a commercial record-ing he must figure out what the players have coming in re-use fees. All of the cartage bills from the people who transport harps, keyboards, percussion equipment, guitar equipment to the ses-sions went to Patti, who then arranged for payment. She was also the official timekeeper during the recording sessions. The mass of detail was well taken care of.

While all of this was going on I, of course, was well into the writing of the score. I work on eight–stave sketch paper shown here.

Example 7

HENRY MANCINI

"Sketch" does not quite describe what is done here. A "short score," as it is commonly referred to, is a better description.

As shown in examples to follow, everything that the orchestra plays is written down on the "sketch." The difference is that instead of each instrument having its own stave, as on the full orchestral score, on the sketch, sections are combined on one stave. Another difference is that the sketch is in concert key whereas most of us use the transposed method on the full score. The page shown above is one of many configurations that the paper comes in. At times three or four staves are all that are necessary.

Some composers of theatrical films have done their own orchestrations. In television, with half–hour and one–hour shows, because of the shortage of time and because of the budget, the composer and orchestrator are lumped into one. Since the orchestras used are not large, he can, or must, go directly to the full score. Since "The Thorn Birds" was a class act, I brought in a man who has been with me since "Breakfast at Tiffany's," Jack Hayes. Jack has worked with just about every major composer going back to Alfred Newman and Victor Young. He is also a fine composer, and at both jobs is first–rate.

With me, Jack's job does not make full use of all his skills as an orchestrator. However, some composers, for one reason or another, do not, or cannot, give him much to go on. He has been given a single line and been asked to "give me two minutes of 'stealth'," based on the line. More than many times he has been called in to assist someone who is brought in to "write" a score, and who has never scored a picture. To cap it off, sometimes the someone can neither read music nor write it down on paper. For obvious reasons, he is referred to as a "hummer." In true fact, Jack uses all of his skills to bail him out.

As Jack finished his full scores he turned over both his score and my sketch to the next link in our chain, the copyist. Joel Franklin is in charge of the copying department at Warner Bros. His staff of copyists do their work in a not–too–large room on the studio lot. The room also serves as the music library for a good deal of the music that has been written at Warner Bros. over the years. The presence of the masters Steiner and Korngold can be felt.

Joel, also, has a master list of the cues in the film. As the scores come in he checks them off as having been completed. He notes exactly the instrumentation of each piece and enters it into a master orchestra breakdown chart.

Example 8

DATE Nov. 30, 1982   CONDUCTOR Henry Mancini   COMPOSER Henry Mancini   INSTRUMENT CHART   (Tuesday A.M.)   SHOW THE THORN BIRDS   #167601 First Episode

CUE NO.	ORIGINAL CUE NO.	SHOW NO.	TITLE — Fair Music	COMPOSER	ORIGINAL TIME	THIS USAGE	PICC	CLAR	CLAR	CORNETS	TROMB	PERC HNS		TUBA			SN DR	BS DR	CYMB	ACCORD	KYBD	GUIT	FIDDLE		TOTAL ORCHESTRA
✓	12A		Fair Music — Click Go The Shears			24	1	1	1	2	1	2		1			1	1	1	−	−	−	−	82 30	11a
✓	18B		A Little Fair Music		5:45	72											SIT DOWN DRS	Glock			Yamaha muted			82 31	3
✓	18C		More Fair Music			40											Drs.	Glock			Yamab muted			82 32	3
✓	28		Tune Up At Drogheda / Drogheda			−				1				1			−			1	−	1/1 lbs	1	82 42	7
✓	29		Party Time		1:24	37				1				1			Drs			1	Pno	Bjo	1	82 43	7
✓	31		Mary's Waltz		3:57	176				1				1			Drs			1	Pno	Bjo	1	82 45	7
✓	32		Kangaroo Trot		1:45	40				1				1			Drs			1	Pno	Bjo	1	82 46	7
✓	33		Drogheda / The Drogheda Drag		1:08	34				1				1			Drs			1	Pno	Bjo	1	82 47	7
✓	34		Dancing / The Dancing Priest		1:15	28				1				1			Drs			1	Pno	Bjo	1	82 48	7
✓	36		Good Night Ladies		:41	16				1				1			Drs			1	Pno	Bjo	1	82 50	7

By cross–checking with Patti DeCaro, Joel made sure that the players called matched with his master list.

He then sent a copy of my sketch to Jay Smith. The sketch contained all the information that he would need to set the film up for recording, i. e., timing, clicks, streamers, etc. If I had made any mistakes in my timings, I would soon receive a call from Jay. Nobody's perfect!

I always conduct from my original sketches. Jack, with the full score, sits in the booth with the recording mixer. Since the entire score had been proof–read, copying errors were minimal. Because Jack was familiar with the score, and the mixer was hearing it for the first time, Jack was able to be of great assistance in the booth. Also in the booth for all twenty–five sessions was producer Stan Margulies. His presence was helpful and welcome.

The music scoring stage at Warner Bros. Studios has a history that goes back to the very beginning of recorded music in films. It is a large room capable of handling orchestras up to ninety–five men. The room was ideally suited for my orchestra and for the type of music that I was writing.

Bobby Fernandez was our music–mixer on the entire film. We met and discussed what format we would be using. The room had a good, comfortable, natural sound.

The score called for an open sound. Since most of the music had little brass or percussion, two prime "leakers" on to the other tracks, Bobby was able to place the microphones a bit further away from the players. He also had hung several "overall" mikes. This added to the ambience I felt the sound needed.

In television most hour– and half–hour shows record their music on three–track 35 mm. magnetic tape. Time and budget dictate this procedure. In other words, the balance you hear on the three–track playback is the final mix. I decided to record 24–track and then personally mix down to the three tracks that would be monaural in the final print. I had much more control with this system, but it consumed countless hours of mixdown time after the orchestra had left. It was worth the effort.

Some ask, "Why bother with all of that detail when most television sets are capable of transmitting only a small part of it through their tiny speakers?"

My answer to this is: No matter whether the music is to be heard on a 1955 Zenith or in a theatre complete with six–track Dolby stereophonic wrap–around sound, personal pride in one's work is involved. There is new hope for sound–conscience television viewers in the form of sets coming out equipped with good speakers _and_ stereo sound.

All that remains now is to conduct the music in sync with the picture. The means by which this is accomplished are varied. One is the clock, a large one with easily readable numbers. The clock has a sweep hand and numbers at every five–second point. One time around totals one minute. Each sequence begins and ends with a streamer. Within the cue you may place streamers wherever you feel you need a sync point. On the sketch the timing at which the streamer hits the right edge of the screen is enclosed by a box or circle. When using the clock (free timing) these lines are indispensable. Click tracks, both constant and variable, are used when the situation calls for them. Chases, fights or any other kinds of scenes that maintain a constant pulse would be very difficult to score without clicks. Combinations of free–timing and the click track are also possible. Starting with clicks you may feel that, at a certain point, the mood and tempo of the scene change. On your sketch you indicate at that certain point the clicks will stop. From there on you proceed with the clock. I prefer the free–timing, clicks and streamer method.

Another method, referred to as the "Newman" system, invented by film composer, Alfred Newman, eliminates the use of the clock altogether. Through a series of visual aids on the film itself the conductor finds his checkpoints. Punches, which are tiny flashes of light produced by the music editor actually perforating the film, guide the conductor through the cue. They can indicate the beginning of each bar or whatever information the composer feels is necessary. Streamers and clicks can also be incorporated into this system.

3 OCTAVES
HARP
BSN
HENRY MANCINI
HARP
HARMONIUM

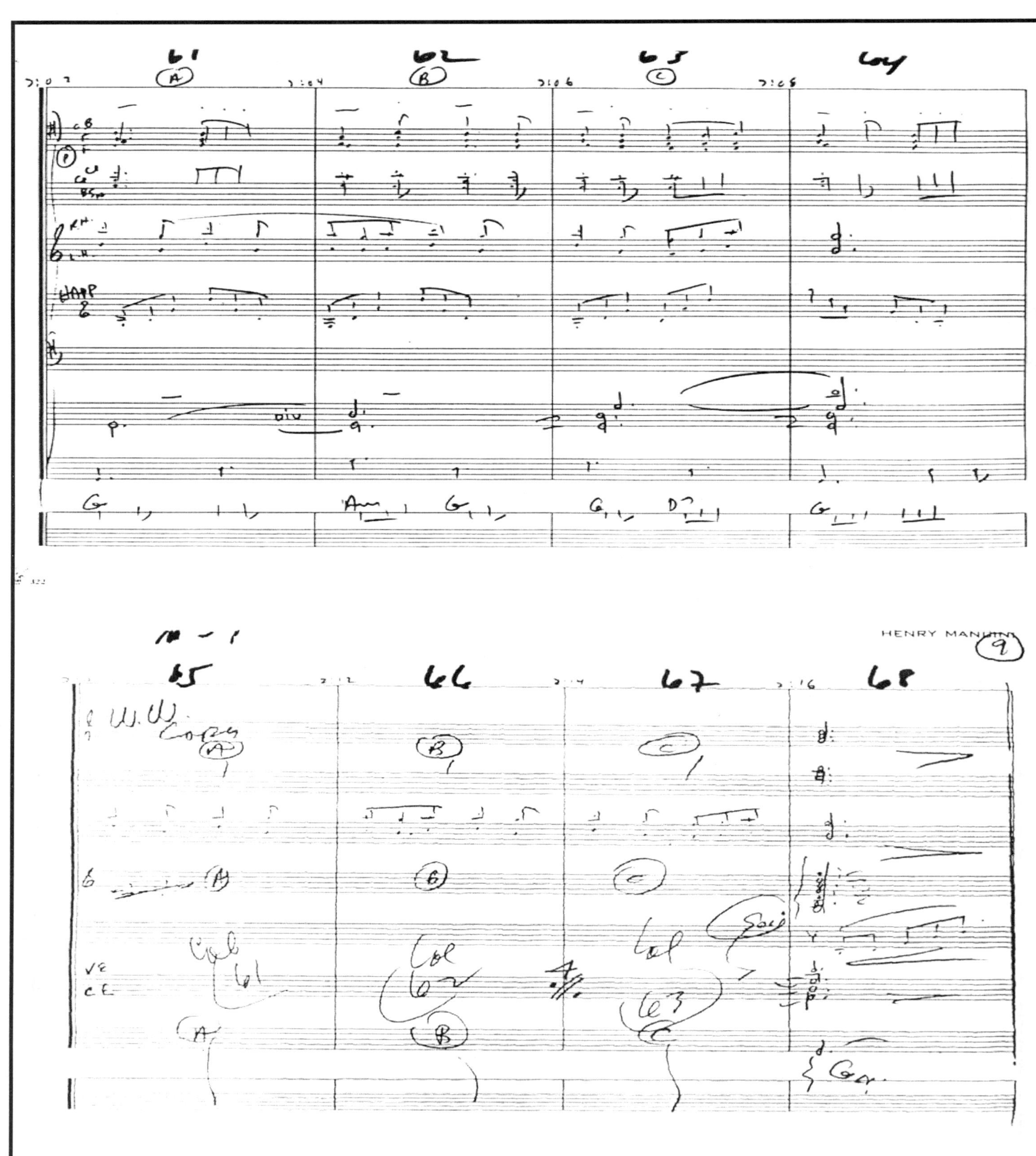

HENRY MANCINI
HARP
DIV
G   Am   G   G   D7   G

The first run-through of a cue is an orientation trip. The composer hears for the first time, live, what he has been carrying around in his head for so long. The music-mixer begins his balance. The players get the feeling of the music. The subsequent playings sort out matters of interpretation. The composer is getting familiar with the timing of the music, trying to get a flowing orchestral performance out of all the impersonal technical work that went into setting the music down on paper. I have found that many of the young writers get so wrapped up in "numbers" that they forget that the real name of the game is "music."

When everything has been sorted out a rehearsal with the film is called for. Of all the steps in the film composing process, this is the time I most enjoy; the first playing of the music with the film. If everything comes together perfectly, it is a high of the first order. Granted, at times, adjustments must be made. A few other times it was back to the drawing board. Accentuating the positive, it is a moment well worth waiting for.

The recording then began. Jay Smith sat at a table behind the podium. He had control of starting and stopping the clock. He also had the job of vocally "slating" (identifying) each take of each cue as we went along. As we recorded I listened to playbacks of all of the cues and noted the accepted takes. We would also listen to playbacks with the dialogue, in order to check how the music played at the lower level. I heard them off the 24-track machine so that I could check at any point whether or not everything was on the track. Incidentally, a three-track 35 mm. magnetic tape is run along with the 24-track. This acts as a safety should we have any kind of a problem with the 24-track later.

I look forward to the mix-down sessions. After the pressure of recording I enjoy sitting down with the mixer and listening to everything once again. I sit, sketch in hand, and cue him as to what is happening as he mixes. We have to be very careful not to mix down with the speakers at too high a level. Things that stand out at a high level have a way of disappearing when the level is dropped. "The Thorn Birds" music was mixed down from the 24-track to 35 mm. three-track. The three-track is tape-coated, sprocketed film to insure perfect sync later when all of the sound elements are combined in the dubbing room.

The music had been recorded without echo. Because of Bobby's adroit placement of the microphone, both close and overall, the music had the open sound I had sought. The proper use of echo is very important to the underscoring. In this case it was used sparingly, mainly to enhance the sound. All of the source music was mixed down without echo. To have echo on the band playing for Mary Carson's party would have been totally disorienting. We would have been seeing 1920 and hearing 1983.

Upon completion of the mix-down, the music tracks were ready for the final phase, dubbing.

DUBBING

At this point, real life takes over. The euphoria of the scoring stage playback, with its large speakers is history. The music will now become part of the overall sound of the film.

Of the three sound elements in a picture, dialogue, music and sound effects, the dialogue is the prime concern. A great deal of time is spent to insure that every word spoken on the screen is clearly audible. The music and sound effects must take their proper place in relation to the dialogue. Stan Margulies supervised the dubbing (also referred to a re-recording).

The dubbing room is actually a small theatre containing a full-sized screen on one wall and a large mixing panel facing the screen. Our film had a three-man crew at the panel, one of whom was handling music tracks. All of the sound tracks are fed into the mixing panel from an adjoining room. The film is mixed one reel at a time (1,000 feet). In earlier years, you had to complete an entire reel to achieve a "take." If a cue was missed at, say 750 feet, you had to start from the beginning of the reel and do it all over again. Today, by means of a system call "rock and roll" you need only replay the mis-cue and insert the correction. The system also makes it possible to run the film forward or backward at high speed.

Many a composer's heart has been broken in this room. Cries of "How can 'they' do this to my music?" have been heard every working day of the week. "They" certainly can and, every so often, do. Depending on the policy of the producer or director, the composer is usually welcome to attend the dubbing sessions. Since I was still writing the next episode while they were dubbing the previous one, I didn't have the time to spend there. Having spent time at all of the recording sessions, Stan was very familiar with the music. It turned out to be one of the best music dubbing jobs I have ever heard on one of my scores.

Part II
The Music

THE MUSIC

The remainder of this book will be taken up by music selected from all four episodes. Detailed timings, sketches and commentary on both will seek to illustrate what the thinking process was behind the music.

The abbreviations used in the timing sheets are as follows:

CS	Close Shot
CU	Close Up
FS	Full Shot
LS	Long Shot
VLS	Very Long Shot
MS	Medium Shot
POV	Point of View
DISS	Dissolve
EOL	End of Line (Dialogue)

Also, you will notice that the timing sheets are calibrated in 1/10 of a second units. My sketches, due to my early work habits, are done in fractions. For example: 1:05.5 on the timing sheet becomes 1:05 1/2 on the sketch. I usually figure the tenths to the nearest half second.

Example 1
M-1 Main Title (Episode I)
⊙ CD Track 1

The Main Title of "The Thorn Birds" is exceptionally long (4:13) and contains thirty title cards. My earlier decision to have a theme with several varied parts paid off here.

I decided that starting the film off with just the dulcimer drone would be unique and effective. In order not to interrupt the flow of the piece I did not emphasize any of the title cards. I also disregarded all cuts and dissolves. This approach, of course, doesn't always apply, but when it does, it's the answer to a composer's prayer.

My click track (four clicks in :04 seconds) is necessary because of the light rhythmic nature of the theme. To hold a tempo steady over such a long piece without clicks was asking for trouble.

At 2:18, to offer some relief from the constant rhythm of the guitars and basses, I let the strings carry on alone until 2:34. The rhythm then starts up again, thus giving the music an effective push forward.

As the car pulls up to the house I change the mood by dropping the clicks and proceeding at a slightly slower, rubato tempo until the end of the cue.

Throughout all of the following music examples, the basses are written one octave above where they sound.

Production: **THE THORNBIRDS**   Production #: 167601
Cue: **M - 1 "MAIN TITLE"**
Begins at **d1:02:04:18**

ABS SMPTE #(df)	REL. TIME:	
		MAIN TITLE
d1:02:04:18	0:00.00	MUSIC BEGINS IN FS - CAMERA PANNING OVER RANCH DROGHEDA
d1:02:06:01	0:01.43	CAMERA REVEALS SHEEP WALKING IN THE FIELD
d1:02:24:17	0:19.99	WE SEE CAR (RALPH) OFF IN THE DISTANCE DRIVING TOWARD CAMERA

d1:02:31:00	0:26.43		MAIN TITLE FADE IN
d1:02:31:16	0:26.96		FADE IN FULL
d1:02:36:04	0:31.58		MAIN TITLE FADE OUT
d1:02:36:07	0:31.67		MAIN TITLE FULL FADE OUT
d1:02:37:22	0:33.17	CUT	FS - RALPH'S CAR DRIVING TOWARD CAMERA
d1:02:46:09	0:41.74		CAMERA FOLLOWS CAR DRIVING AWAY
d1:02:54:20	0:50.12	CUT	CS - RALPH AT THE WHEEL
d1:02:56:11	0:51.82		RICHARD CHAMBERLAIN CREDIT FADE IN
d1:02:59:07	0:54.69		AND START FADE OUT
d1:02:59:14	0:54.92		FULL FADE OUT
d1:03:01:15	0:56.89	CUT	LS - SIDE ANGLE OF RALPH'S CAR DRIVING
d1:03:01:23	0:57.16		RACHEL WARD CREDIT FADE IN
d1:03:04:04	0:59.53		AND START FADE OUT
d1:03:04:10	0:59.73		FULL FADE OUT
d1:03:05:23	1:01.16		FADE IN JEAN SIMMONS CREDIT
d1:03:08:04	1:03.53		START FADE OUT
d1:03:08:09	1:03.70		FULL FADE OUT
d1:03:09:11	1:04.75		START DISSOLVE
d1:03:10:17	1:05.97		CENTER DISSOLVE IN FS - THE PLAINS
d1:03:11:28	1:07.33		END DISSOLVE IN LS - RALPH DRIVING TOWARD CAMERA
d1:03:16:14	1:11.87		FADE IN KEN HOWARD CREDIT AS CAMERA SLOWLY PANS LEFT OVER THE GATE TO DROGHEDA
d1:03:18:23	1:14.17		START FADE OUT
d1:03:18.28	1:14.34		FULL FADE OUT
d1:03:20.13	1:15.84		FADE IN MARE WINNINGHAM CREDIT
d1:03:22:28	1:18.35		FULL FADE OUT AS RALPH DRIVES TOWARD THE GATE
d1:03:24:14	1:19.88		FADE IN PIPER LAURIE CREDIT
d1:03:26:10	1:21.75		RALPH STOPS AT THE GATE
d1:03:26:24	1:22.22		PIPER LAURIE CREDIT STARTS TO FADE
d1:03:26:29	1:22.38		FULL FADE OUT
d1:03:27:25	1:23.25	CUT	MS - RALPH IN THE CAR PULLING UP THE HAND BRAKE
d1:03:29:23	1:25.19		FADE IN RICHARD KILEY CREDIT AS RALPH OPENS THE DOOR
d1:03:30:28	1:26.35		RALPH STEPS OUT OF CAR
d1:03:32:02	1:27.49		AND PUSHES ON THE DOOR AS RICHARD KILEY CREDIT STARTS TO FADE
d1:03:32:10	1:27.75		FULL FADE OUT AS RALPH LOOKS OFF STAGE

d1:03:32:13	1:27.85		RALPH LOOKS OFF STAGE
d1:03:32:15	1:27.92		CAR DOOR IS SHUT TIGHT
d1:03:33:21	1:29.12	CUT	FS - KANGAROO JUMPING AWAY FROM THE CAMERA
d1:03:39:25	1:35.26	CUT	MS - RALPH WATCHING KANGAROO
d1:03:40:24	1:36.23		CAMERA FOLLOWS RALPH WALKING FORWARD TOWARD THE GATE
d1:03:42:13	1:37.86		FADE IN EARL HOLLIMAN CREDIT
d1:03:44:24	1:40.23		START FADE OUT
d1:03:45:00	1:40.43		FULL FADE OUT
d1:03:46:15	1:41.94		RALPH OPENS THE GATE AS BRYAN BROWN CREDIT FADES IN
d1:03:48:24	1:44.24		START FADE OUT AS RALPH GIVES THE GATE A PUSH
d1:03:49:01	1:44.47		FULL FADE OUT AS RALPH WALKS AWAY FROM THE GATE
d1:03:50:13	1:45.87		START FADE IN PHILLIP ANGLIM
d1:03:52:01	1:47.47		RALPH OPENS THE CAR DOOR
d1:03:52:25	1:48.27		HE STEPS UP INTO THE CAR
d1:03:53:01	1:48.31		START FADE OUT
d1:03:54:01	1:48.48		FULL FADE OUT
d1:03:54:11	1:49.48		AND SITS DOWN
d1:03:54:13	1:49.88		RALPH PULLS ON THE DOOR
d1:03:54:20	1:50.11		CHRISTOPHER PLUMMER CREDIT FADES IN
d1:03:56:26	1:52.31		RALPH SHUTS THE DOOR
d1:03:57:01	1:52.48		CREDIT BEGINS TO FADE
d1:03:57:27	1:53.35		FULL FADE OUT
d1:03:58:24	1:54.25		AND DRIVES TOWARD THE GATE
d1:03:59:11	1:54.81		START DISSOLVE
d1:04:00:08	1:55.85		CENTER DISSOLVE IN FS - DRIVING TOWARD CAMERA
d1:04:05:05	2:00.55		BARBARA STANWYCK CREDIT FADE IN
d1:04:07:21	2:03.09		FULL FADE OUT
d1:04:10:07	2:05.63		START DISSOLVE
d1:04:11:05	2:06.56		CENTER DISSOLVE IN MS - RALPH'S CAR DRIVING TOWARD CAMERA
d1:04:11:25	2:07.23		END DISSOLVE
d1:04:15:26	2:11.26		CAMERA SLOWLY PANS LEFT
d1:04:16:18	2:12.00		CAMERA REVEALS SHEEP - RALPH DRIVES TOWARD SHEEP
d1:04:18:15	2:13.90		START FADE IN JOHN FRIEDRICH CREDIT
d1:04:20:26	2:16.27		START FADE OUT
d1:04:21:02	2:16.47		FULL FADE OUT

d1:04:22:15	2:17.90		START FADE IN ALLYN MCLERIE CREDIT
d1:04:33:03	2:28.52		FULL FADE OUT
d1:04:24:26	2:20.27		START FADE OUT
d1:04:25:02	2:20.47		FULL FADE OUT
d1:04:26:15	2:21.91		FADE IN RICHARD VENTURE CREDIT
d1:04:28:28	2:24.34		CREDIT STARTS TO FADE
d1:04:29:04	2:24.54		FULL FADE OUT
d1:04:30:15	2:25.91		FADE IN STEPHANIE FARACY CREDIT
d1:04:32:27	2:28.31		START FADE OUT
d1:04:34:15	2:29.92		RALPH DRIVES AWAY FROM THE SHEEP AS BARRY CORBIN CREDIT FADES IN
d1:04:36:27	2:32.32		START FADE OUT
d1:04:37:02	2:32.49		FULL FADE OUT
d1:04:39:08	2:34.69		START DISSOLVE
d1:04:40:11	2:35.79		CENTER DISSOLVE IN FS - HILLS
d1:04:41:12	2:36.82		END DISSOLVE
d1:04:42:03	2:37.52		RALPH'S CAR DRIVES INTO VIEW TOWARD THE CAMERA
d1:04:43:25	2:39.26		SYDNEY PENNY CREDIT FADES IN
d1:04:46:06	2:41.62		CREDITS STARTS TO FADE
d1:04:46:13	2:41.86		CREDIT FULL OUT
d1:04:47:25	2:43.26		TWO MORE CREDITS FADE IN
d1:04:50:05	2:45.60		CREDITS START TO FADE AS RALPH PASSES IN FRONT OF THE CAMERA
d1:04:50:14	2:45.90		CREDITS FULL OUT
d1:04:51:24	2:47.23	CUT	MS - OVER RALPH'S SHOULDER LOOKING THRU WINDSHIELD - DRIVING TOWARD TWO FARM HANDS
d1:04:53:24	2:49.24		FADE IN ON HENRY MANCINI CREDIT
d1:04:56:02	2:51.50		CREDIT STARTS TO FADE
d1:04:56:11	2:51.81		CREDIT FULL OUT
d1:04:57:27	2:53.34		RALPH SALUTES THE TWO FARM HANDS

The Thorn Birds Theme

Main Title

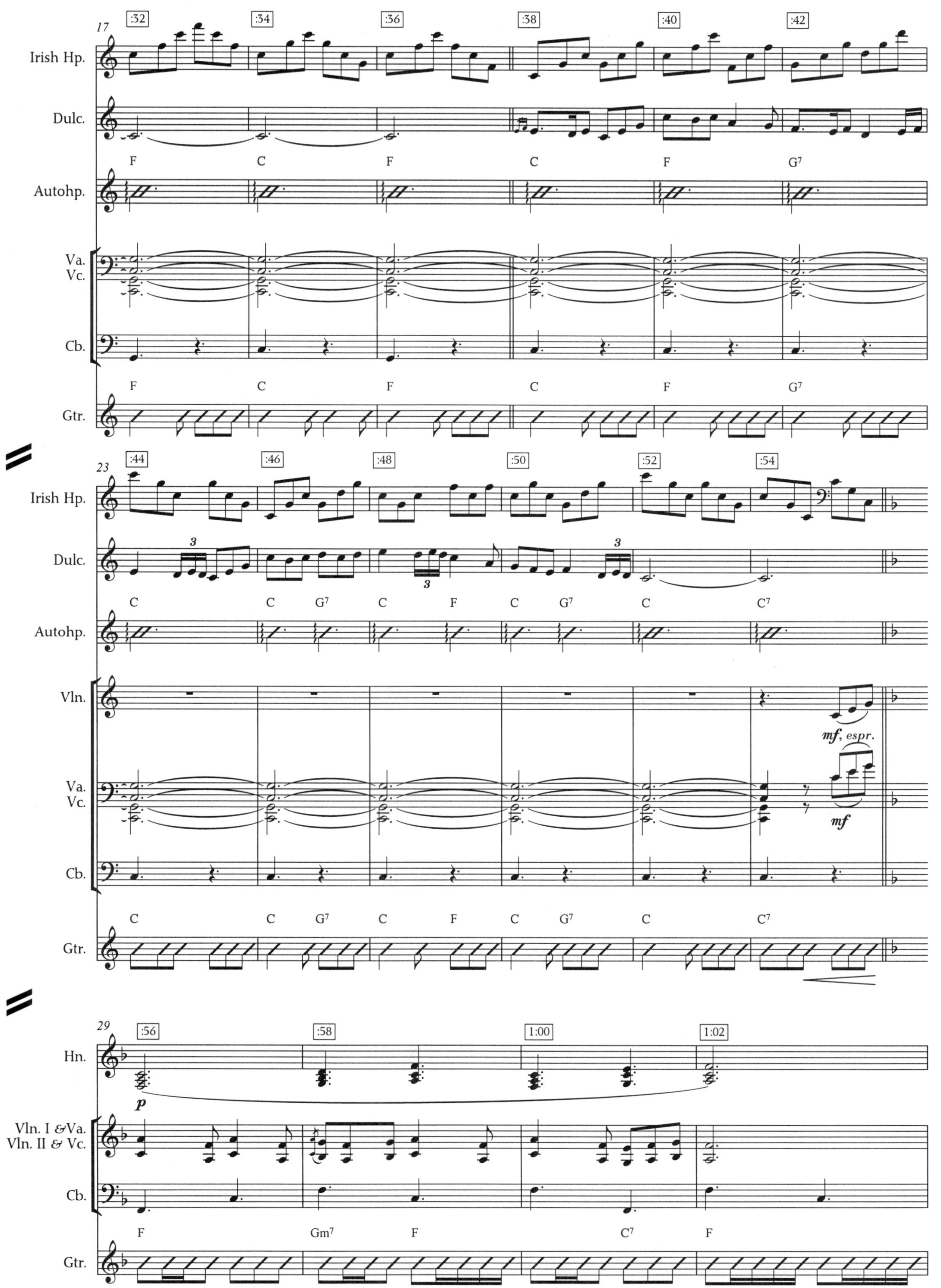
Irish Hp.
Dulc.
Autohp.
Va.
Vc.
Cb.
Gtr.
Vln.
Hn.
Vln. I & Va.
Vln. II & Vc.

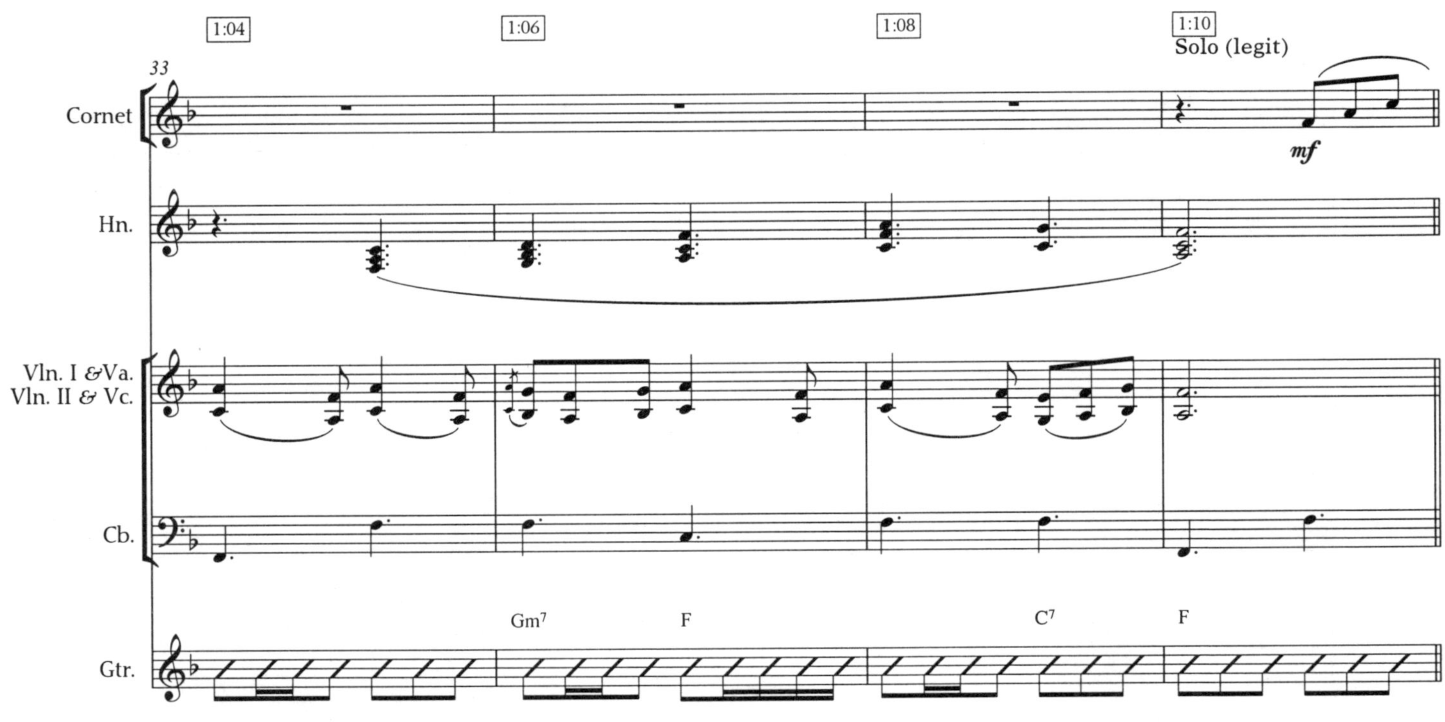
1:04
1:06
1:08
1:10
Solo (legit)
33
Cornet
mf
Hn.
Vln. I &Va.
Vln. II & Vc.
Cb.
Gm7
F
C7
F
Gtr.

1:12
1:14
1:16
1:18
1:20
1:22
1:24
1:26
37
F scale
Hp.
gliss.
Cnt.
3
Vln.
p
Va.
Vc.
div.
2 arco
2 pizz.
Cb.
Bb
C7
F
Dm
Gm
F
Bb
C7
F
Dm
Gm
F
Gtr.

1:28
1:30
1:32
1:34
45
a3
Hn.
mp
3 Tbn.:
mp
Tbn.
Tba.
Tba: p
Song Bells
Vln.
mf
Va.
Vc.
mf
Tutti, pizz.
Cb.
F
Gm
F
C
F
Gtr.
1:36
1:38
1:40
1:42
49
Fl. a2,
2Fl.
Ob.
Ob.
Cl. 1
2 Cl.
Bsn.
Cl. 2,
Bsn.
mf
mf
(a3)
Hn.
Tbn.
Tba.
Song Bells
Vln.
Va.
Vc.
Cb.
Gm
F
Gm
C7
F
Gtr.

1:44
1:46
1:48
1:50
53
2 Fl.
Ob.
2 Cl.
Bsn.
Hp.
Vln.
Va.
Vc.
p
p
Cb.
D
G
A7
D
Gtr. 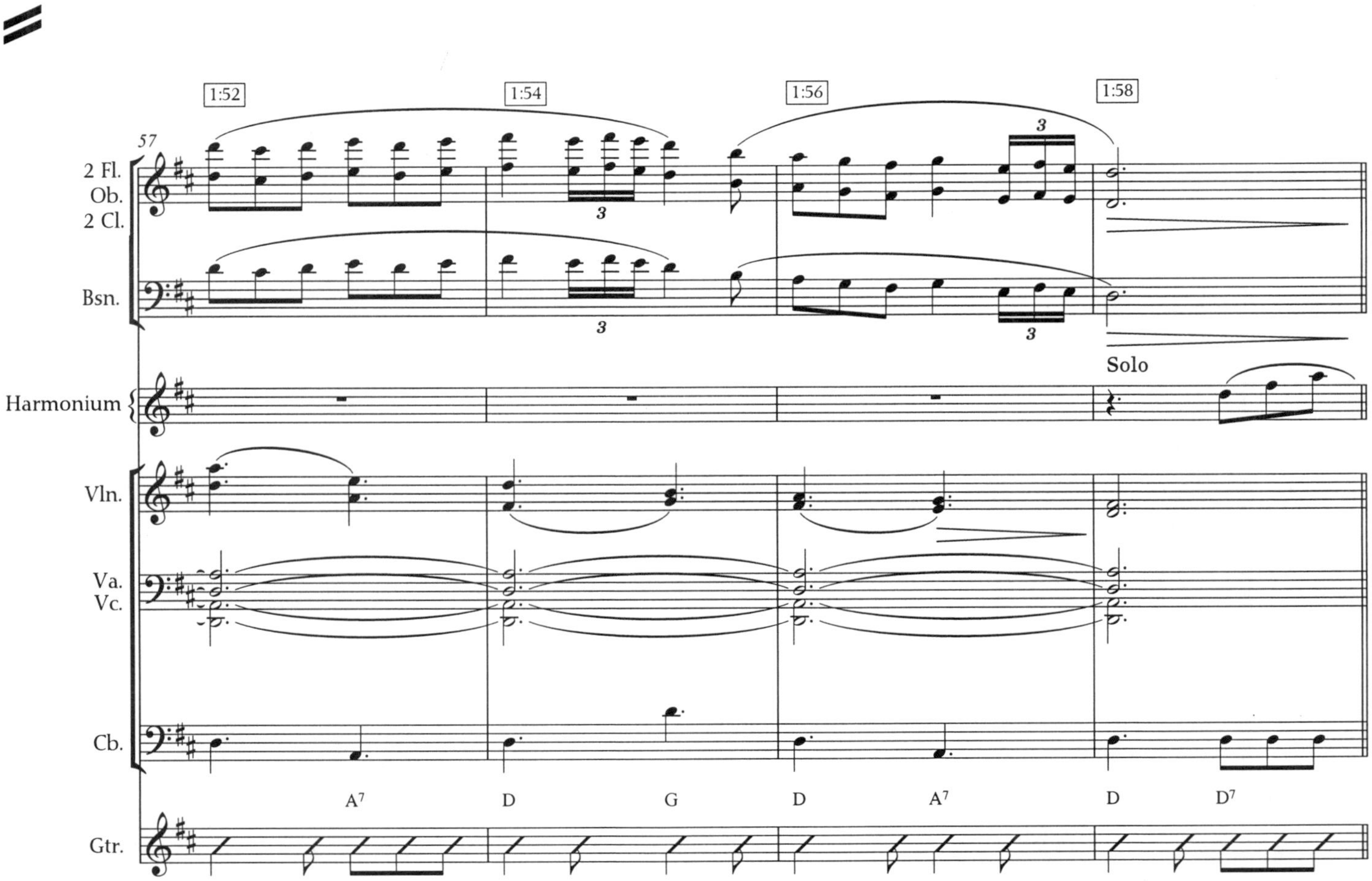
3
3
3
1:52
1:54
1:56
1:58
57
2 Fl.
Ob.
2 Cl.
Bsn.
Harmonium
Solo
Vln.
Va.
Vc.
Cb.
A7
D
G
D
A7
D
D7
Gtr.
3
3
3
3

2:00
2:02
2:04
2:06
61 Ob.
2Fl.
Ob.
2 Fl.
p
2 Cl.
Bsn.
p
Hp.
Harm.
div.
Va.
Vc.
div.
Cb.
G
Am
G
D7
G
Gtr.
2:08
2:10
2:12
2:14
65
(Ob.
2Fl.
Ob.
Fl.)
2 Cl.
Bsn.
Hp.
Harm.
Vln.
Soli
Va.
Vc.
div.
unis.
div.
Cb.
G
Am
G
D7
G
Gtr.

2:16
2:18
2:20
2:22
69
Vln.
unis.
Va.
Vc.
unis.
3
3

2:24
2:26
2:28
2:30
2:32
2:34
73
Cl. 1, Eng. Hn.
Eng. Hn.
2 Cl.
Bsn.
mf
Cl. 2, Bsn.
a3
1., 2.
Hn.
3.
mf
Vln.
mf
Va.
Vc.
div.
mf
Cb.
G
C
Dm
C
Gtr.

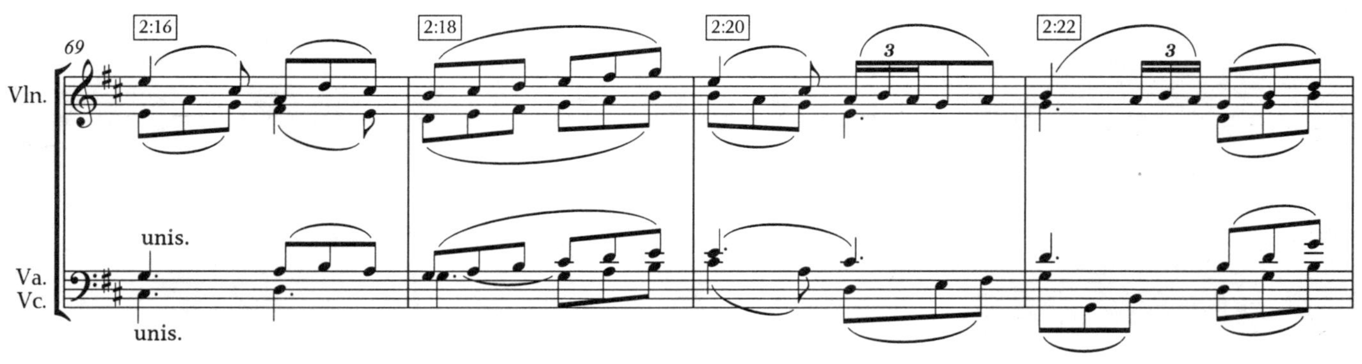

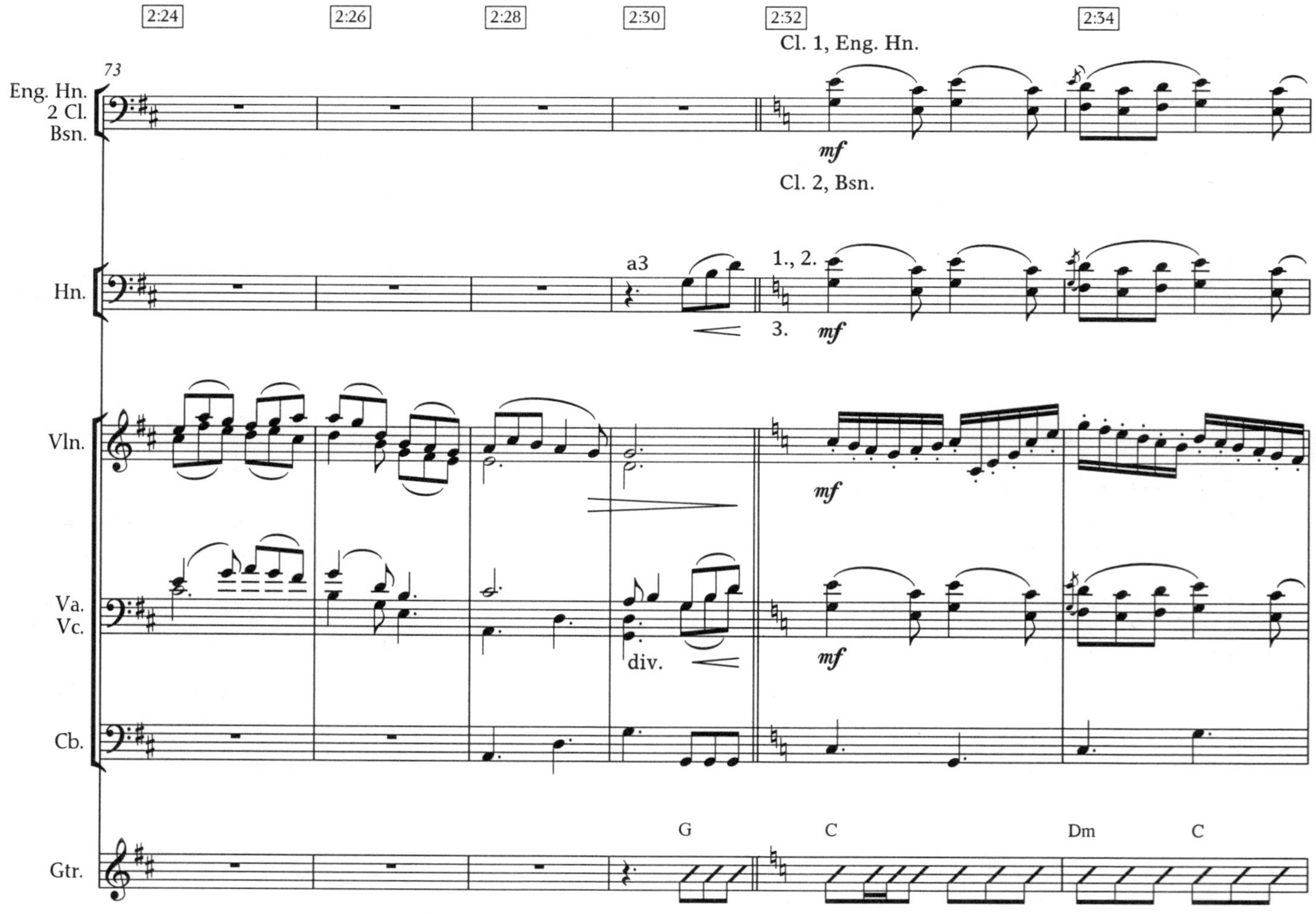

2:36
2:38
2:40
2:42
(Eng. Hn., Cl. 1
79
Eng. Hn.
2 Cl.
Bsn.
Cl. 2, Bsn.)
(1., 2.,
Hn.
3.)
Vln.
Va.
Vc.
Cb.
G7
C
F
C
Gtr.
2:44
2:46
2:48
2:50
2:52
2:54
(Eng. Hn., Cl. 1
83
Eng. Hn.
2 Cl.
Bsn.
Cl. 2, Bsn.)
(1., 2.,
Hn.
3.)
a3
mf
mf
Tbn.
Tba.
p
C scale
gliss.
Hp.
Vln.
legato
Va.
Vc.
3
3
3
Cb.
F
G7
C
F
G7
C
Am
Dm
C
Gtr.

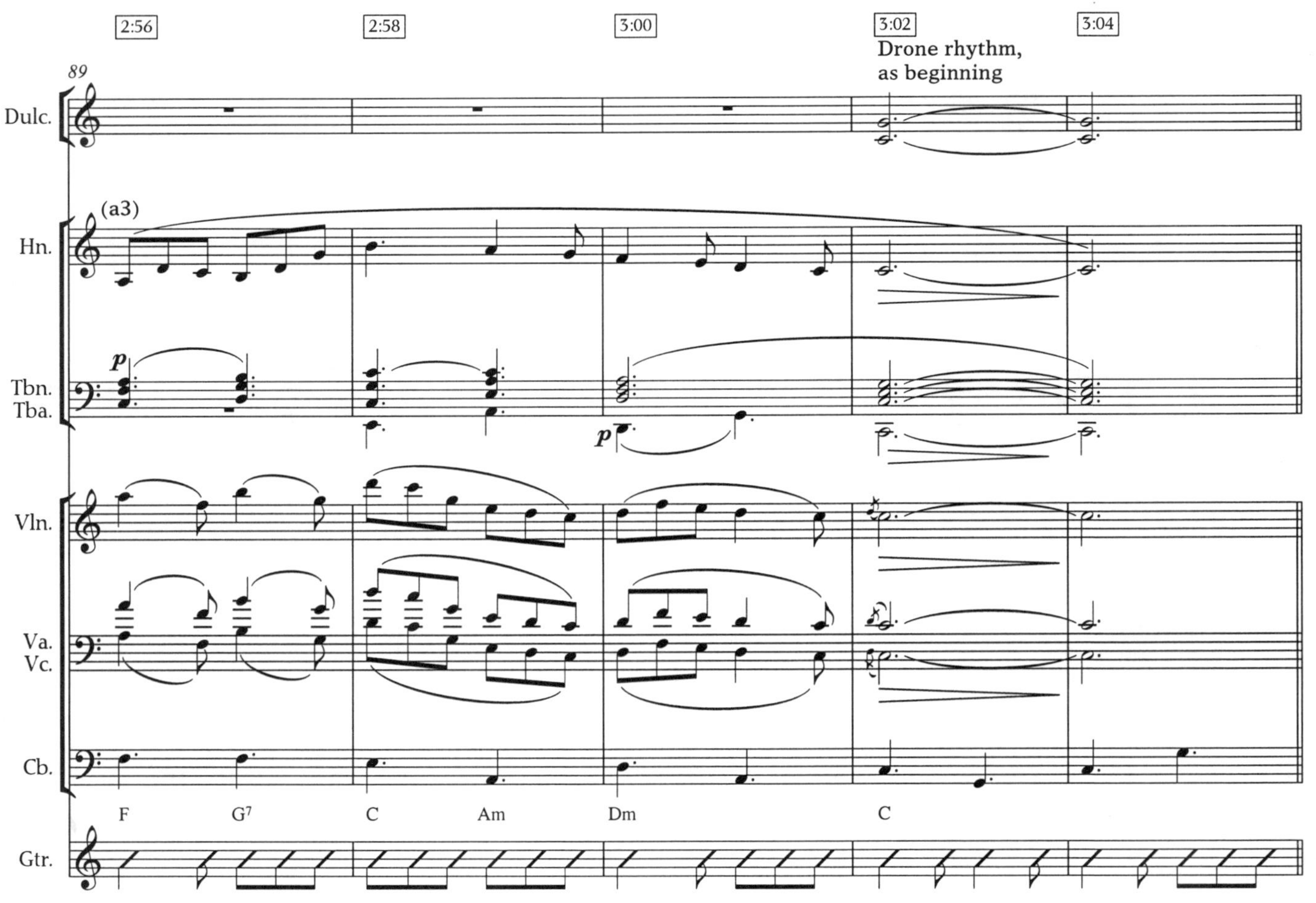
2:56
2:58
3:00
3:02
3:04
Drone rhythm,
as beginning
89
Dulc.
Hn.
(a3)
p
Tbn.
Tba.
p
p
Vln.
Va.
Vc.
Cb.
F
G7
C
Am
Dm
C
Gtr.

3:06
3:08
3:10
3:12
3:14
3:16
94
Dulc.
3
3
C
F
G7
C
G7
C
F
Auto Hp.
Irish Hp.
p
p
p
div.
Va.
Vc.
div.
p
Cb.
C
F
G7
C
G7
C
F
Gtr.

3:18
3:20
3:22
3:24
3:26
3:28
3:30
100
Dulc.
3
3
C
G7
C
G7
C
G7
C
G7
Auto Hp.
Irish Hp.
Vln.
pp
Va.
Vc.
Cb.
C
G7
C
G7
C
G7
C
G7
Gtr.

Clix off
3:32
3:34
3:36
3:39.5
Stop drone rhythm
107
Dulc.
3
3
C
G7
C
Auto Hp.
Hp.
gliss.
Vln.
Va.
Vc.
Cb.
C
G7
C
Gtr.

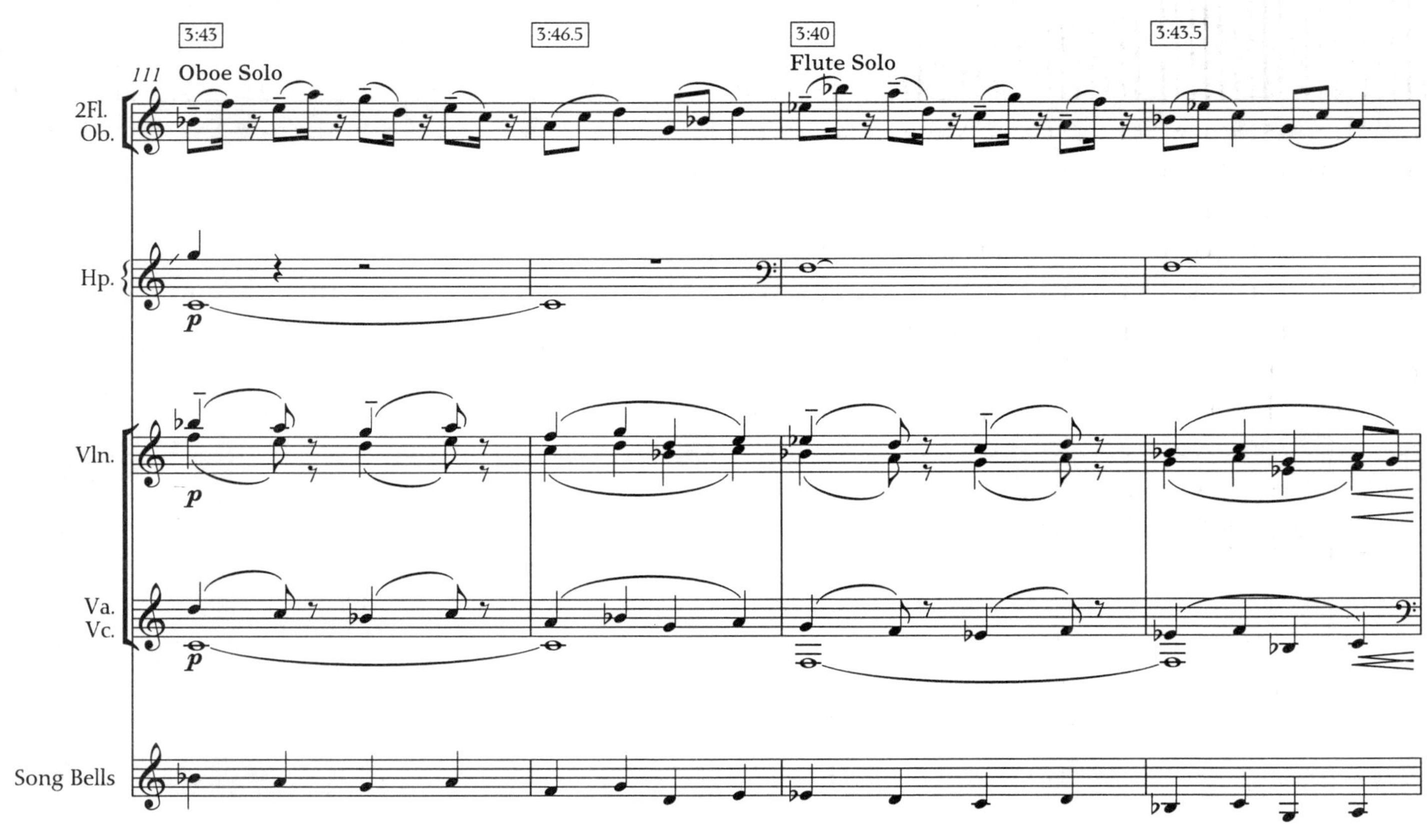
3:43
3:46.5
3:40
3:43.5
111
Oboe Solo
Flute Solo
2Fl.
Ob.
Hp.
p
Vln.
p
Va.
Vc.
p
Song Bells

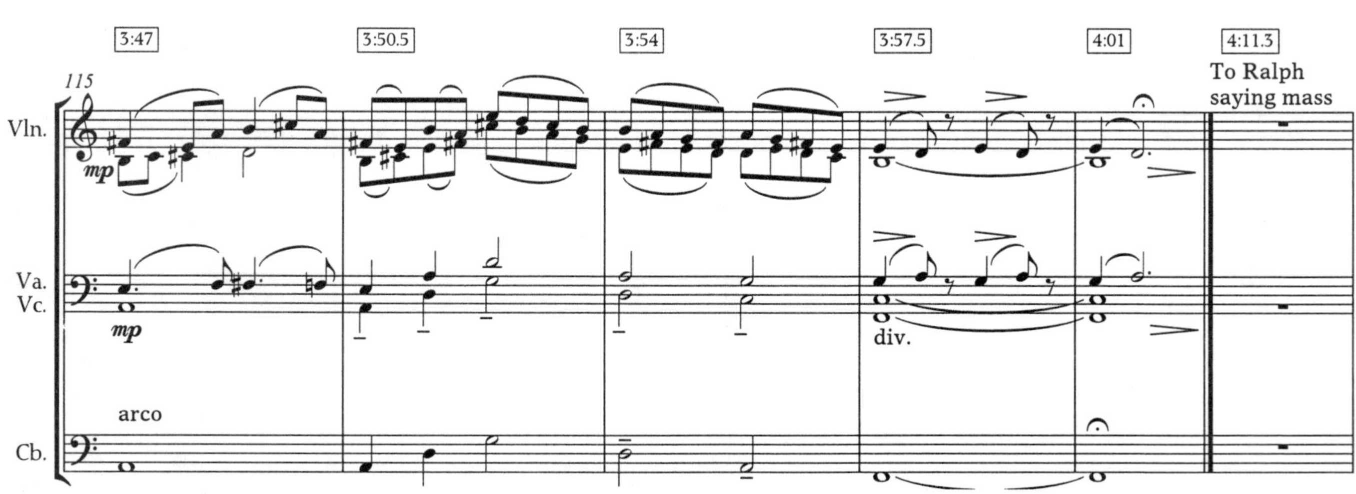
3:47
3:50.5
3:54
3:57.5
4:01
4:11.3
115
To Ralph
saying mass
Vln.
mp
Va.
Vc.
mp
div.
arco
Cb.

Example 2
M–7 Awestruck Meggie (Episode I)
⊙ CD Track 2

The first complete use of "Meggie's Theme" occurs as Meggie, as a child, approaches the large, impressive wool shed. She is fascinated by the sight. Throughout the film this will be her sanctuary, her very own private place.

The first two bars are an introductory motif based on the first two chords of the theme. Although the orchestration calls for the celesta to carry this line, throughout the score it re–occurs in various keys and registers of the orchestra. The rolling eighth–note line will become an integral part of the theme as the film progresses.

The celesta, Irish harp, song bells and muted strings create an ethereal atmosphere.

Production: **THE THORNBIRDS**   Production #: **167601**
Cue: **M - 7 REVISED "AWESTRUCK MEGGIE"**
Begins at **d0:00:00:00**

ABS SMPTE #(df)	REL. TIME:		
d0:00:00:00	0:00.00		START MUSIC ON CUT TO MEGGIE WALKING TOWARD CAMERA CARRYING A MILK CAN
	0:03.6		SHE SLOWS HER PACE AS SHE SEES SOMETHING OFF-CAMERA
	0:12.8		SHE STOPS IN FRONT OF CAMERA LOOKING WITH CURIOUSITY AT THE WOOLSHED
	0:13.8	CUT	MLS OF MEGGIE STANDING AND LOOKING AT THE WOOLSHED IN THE DISTANCE, AS SHE MOVES VERY SLOWLY TOWARDS IT, AND CAMERA PANS OVER TOWARD THE SHED ITSELF
	0:24.4	CUT	MEGGIE WALKING UP THE RAMP. . .
	0:29.2		. . .AND STARTS INTO THE BUILDING, SLOWING HER STEP AS SHE REACTS WITH AWE
	0:32.4		WITHOUT TAKING HER EYES OFF THE INTERIOR, SHE STOPS AND SLOWLY BEGINS TO SET THE MILK CAN DOWN
	0:35.5		SHE CONTINUES ON INTO THE BARN, SLOWLY, DELIBERATELY, AS CAMERA PANS WITH HER
	0:48.6	CUT	A SHOT FROM BEHIND HER, LOOKING OVER HER SHOULDER AS WE SEE HER APPROACHING THE HUGE WINDOW IN THE DISTANCE, THE WHOLE SCENE ALMOST RESEMBLING A HUGE CATHEDRAL
	0:54.0	CUT	LOW-ANGLE CLOSER SHOT AS CAMERA MOVES WITH HER AS SHE CONTINUES TO WALK
	0:58.9	CUT	MLS FROM THE REAR OF THE "CATHEDRAL" AS BEFORE AS SHE CONTINUES TO APPROACH THE LARGE SUNLIT WINDOW IN FRONT OF HER
	1:02.6	CUT	CLOSER SHOT AS SHE CONTINUES TOWARD THE SUNLIT AREA
	1:09.3		SHE PAUSES IN FRONT OF THE LARGE TABLE, AND PUTS HER HAND REVERENTLY ON IT
	1:10.9		SHE STARTS TO WALK THE LENGTH OF IT, RUNNING HER HAND ALONG IT AS SHE GOES
	1:16.9		SHE PAUSES AT THE CORNER OF THE TABLE AND LOOKS UP
	1:20.2	CUT	HER POV: THE BRIGHT LIGHT STREAMING IN THRU THE OVERHEAD WINDOWS

	1:24.2	CUT	CLOSE SHOT OF MEGGIE AS SHE MOVES HER HEAD TO LOOK ACROSS THE LENGTH OF THE CEILING TO THE BARN
END MUSIC	1:28.0	CUT	(CHANGE OF LOCATION): THE CLOCK ON MARY'S MANTEL, AS CAMERA SLOWLY STARTS TO PAN AWAY FROM IT
	1:31.4		AS WE HEAR MARY SAY TO HER LAWYER: "WELL, THE SECURITIES SEEM TO BE HOLDING WELL. . ." ETC.

Awestruck Meggie

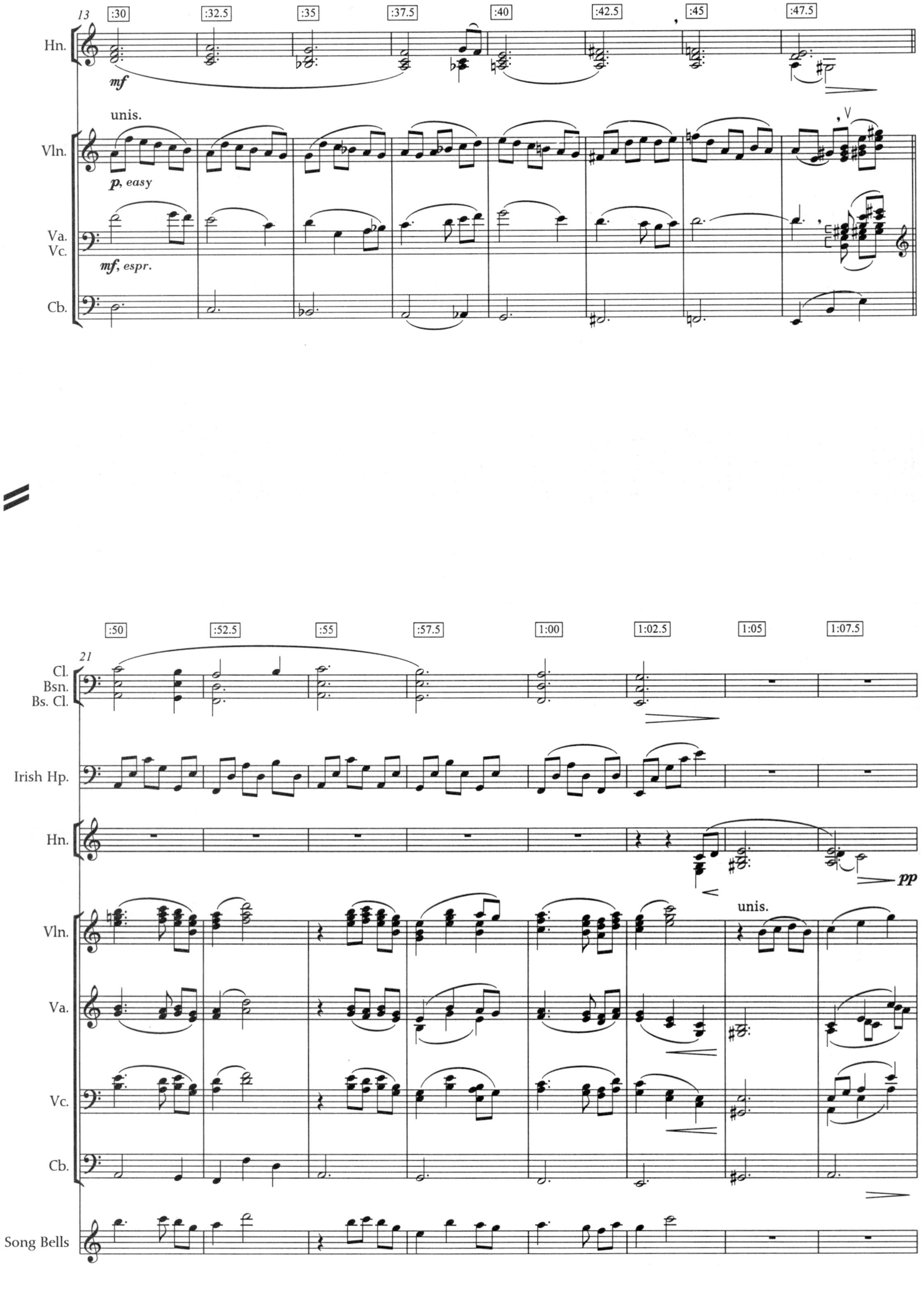
13
:30
:32.5
:35
:37.5
:40
:42.5
:45
:47.5
Hn.
mf
unis.
Vln.
p, easy
Va.
Vc.
mf, espr.
Cb.
21
:50
:52.5
:55
:57.5
1:00
1:02.5
1:05
1:07.5
Cl.
Bsn.
Bs. Cl.
Irish Hp.
Hn.
pp
unis.
Vln.
Va.
Vc.
Cb.
Song Bells

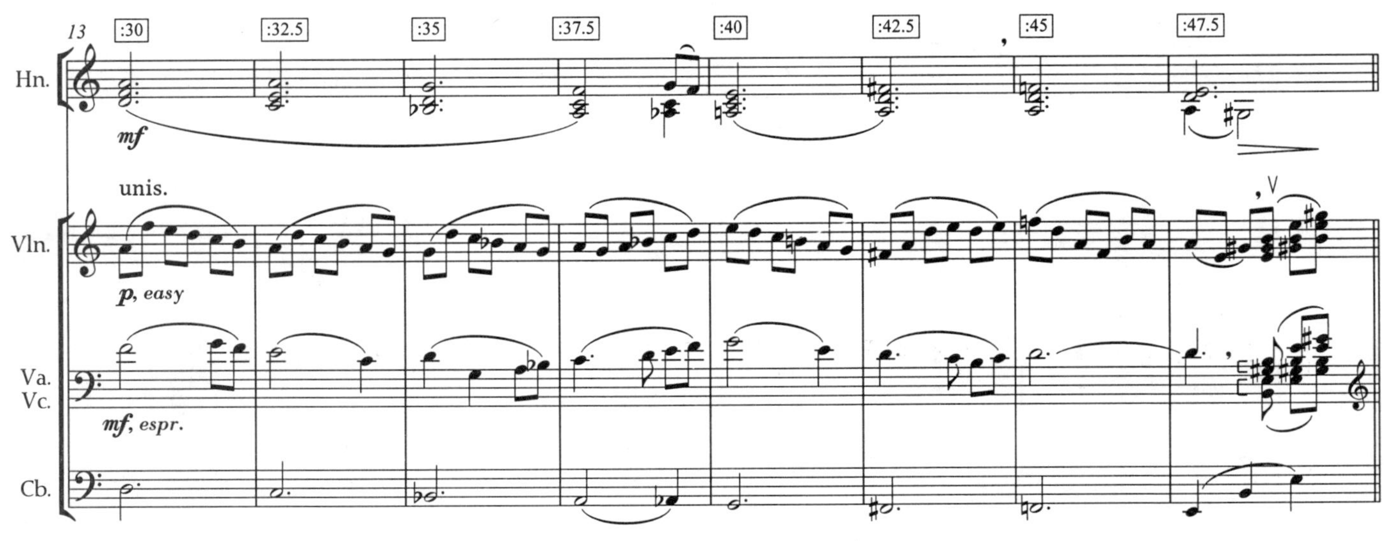

Example 3
M–11 Stuie Grows Up (Episode I)
⊙ **CD Track 3**

The overall effect of this section is one of a gradual crescendo starting from a mezzo piano building to a double forte. The six violas and six celli set up the rustle of impending danger. At :13 seconds the basses, two bass clarinets and bassoon add their ominous line under the violins' entrance. At :38 seconds the animals start their very noisy encounter. Straight muted trumpets and French horns take over a new thought along with the violins. I tried here to create more tension and weight without having it sound like a battle scene from World War II. The muted brass has a certain meanness that is not overpowering. The celli, basses and low piano, in unison, propel us forward with an agitated counterline.

After the boar has finished off the dog, he turns his attention toward Stuie, who is now in real trouble. As Stuie cocks his gun, the moving brass line leads into an ostinato (A), over which the brass builds in string unison lines to the gunshot that end the boar, the cue and the act.

Production: **THE THORNBIRDS**   Production #: 167601
Cue: **M - 11 "STUIE GROWS UP"**
Begins at **d0:00:00:00**

ABS SMPTE #(df)	REL. TIME:		
			PETE HAS JUST BEEN GIVING THE BOYS A LECTURE ABOUT WASTING WATER IN THE OUTBACK, WHEN THE DOG SUDDENLY STARTS BARKING. PETE LOOKS ALL AROUND AND SAYS: **"WHAT IS IT, BOY? WHAT ARE YOU SMELLING NOW?"**
d0:00:00:00	0:00.00		START MUSIC ON AFTER THE ABOVE ON CUT TO THE WILD BOAR STANDING IN A CLEARING
	0:03.1	CUT	PETE AND THE BOYS LOOKING
	0:03.5		ONE OF THE BOYS SAYS: **"WHAT IS THAT THING?"**
	0:04.9		PETE: **"JACK, HOLD THAT DOG."**
	0:06.4	CUT	JACK AS HE STARTS TO MOVE TOWARDS THE DOG

0:07.4		PETE: **"IT'S A WILD PIG. A BOAR."**
0:09.6		THE OTHER BOY STARTS TO STEP FORWARD AS HE SAYS: **"LET'S GET HIM!"**
0:10.3		PETE: **"NO!"**
0:11.1	CUT	EOL. THEIR POV: STU ON HIS HORSE MOVING IN SLOWLY TOWARD THE BOAR
0:13.3	CUT	CLOSER SHOT OF STU ON THE HORSE AS HE WALKS HIS HORSE IN SLOWLY
0:15.3	CUT	MLS OF THE BOAR STANDING IN THE CLEARING
0:17.0	CUT	PETE AND THE BOYS, AS PETE CALLS OUT: **"STEWART, GET DOWN FROM THERE!"**
0:19.1	CUT	EOL. THEIR POV: STU MOVING IN SLOWLY
0:21.0	CUT	PETE AND ONE OF THE BOYS AS THE BOY SAYS: **"I WANT TO SHOOT AT IT!"**
0:21.8		PETE: **"NO!"**
0:22.9		SLIGHT PAUSE, AS HE GRABS THE BOY BY THE SLEEVE AND STOPS HIM
0:23.6		PETE SAYS TO HIM: **"HE'S TOO FAR AWAY. AND IF YOU SHOOT AT A WILD BOAR, BELIEVE ME, YOU'D BETTER KILL HIM! OR HE'LL KILL YOU!"**
0:30.6		EOL, AS THE BOY TURNS TO LOOK AT THE BOAR AGAIN
0:35.4	CUT	PETE AND THE BOYS, AS THE DOG BREAKS AWAY FROM JACK AND STARTS TO RUN TOWARDS THE BOAR
0:37.1		PETE SEES IT AND SAYS: **"DAMN!"**
0:38.0	CUT	EOL. MS AS THE DOG STARTS TO ATTACK THE BOAR. . .
0:39.5		. . .GRABBING HIM BY THE HIND LEG. . .
0:40.7	CUT	PETE AND THE BOYS AS THEY START TOWARDS THE DOG AS PETE SAYS: **"COME ON, LADS. COME ON!"**
0:42.9		EOL, AS HE MOVES TOWARD THE HORSE
0:43.4	CUT	THE DOG AND THE BOAR FIGHTING
0:44.9	CUT	MLS OF STU AS HE STARTS TO GET OFF HIS HORSE
0:48.0		HE STARTS TO DRAW HIS RIFLE OUT OF HIS HOLSTER
0:48.4	CUT	THE BOYS WATCHING AS ONE OF THEM SHOUTS: **"STUIE, NO!"**
0:49.8	CUT	EOL. PETE AT HIS HORSE AS HE LOOKS UP QUICKLY
0:50.4		HE PUTS HIS HAND ON HIS OWN RIFLE
0:50.9	CUT	MS, OF STU, GUN IN HAND, AS HE STARTS TO ADVANCE SLOWLY TOWARD THE BOAT
0:52.8	CUT	THE BOAR AND THE DOG FIGHTING
0:55.1	CUT	STU ADVANCING SLOWLY, HOLDING HIS RIFLE IN FRONT OF HIM
0:57.8	CUT	THE BOAR AS IT RUSHES THE DOG SUDDENLY. . .

0:58.3		...AND GORES IT WITH ITS TUSKS AND TOSSES IT THRU THE AIR AS THE DOG YELPS LOUDLY
0:59.6	CUT	STU, ADVANCING VERY SLOWLY
1:03.0	CUT	CLOSER SHOT OF THE BOAR
1:05.4	CUT	MCU OF STU...
1:06.6		...AS HE COCKS HIS RIFLE
1:08.6	CUT	PETE STANDING NEXT TO HIS HORSE WITH HIS HAND ON HIS RIFLE
1:09.7		HE DRAWS HIS RIFLE OUT SLOWLY
1:13.6	CUT	STU, SLOWLY BRINGING THE GUN SIGHTS UP TO HIS EYE
1:15.3	CUT	MCU OF THE BOAR
1:16.7	CUT	STU WITH HIS RIFLE...
1:17.2		...AS HE STARTS TO LOWER IT SLIGHTLY
1:18.0	CUT	CU OF THE BOAR AS HE SUDDENLY STARTS TO RUN TOWARD STU
1:19.1	CUT	THE BOYS AS ONE OF THEM SAYS **"STUIE!"**
1:20.2	CUT	CU OF STU RAISING THE SIGHTS TO HIS EYE
1:20.9	CUT	HIS POV: THE BOAR RUSHING AT HIM
1:21.7	CUT	CU OF STU AIMING
1:22.8	CUT	HIS POV: THE BOAR COMING CLOSER NOW
1:23.3	CUT	CU OF STU AIMING
1:24.0	CUT	THE BOAR COMING VERY NEAR NOW
1:24.4	CUT	CU OF STU AIMING, AS ONE OF THE BOYS SHOUTS: **"STUIE!"**
1:25.3	END MUSIC	UNDER THE GUNSHOT, IN CUT TO BLACK (COMMERCIAL) (1/2 SECOND BEFORE FULL OUT)

M-11 Episode I

Stuie Grows Up

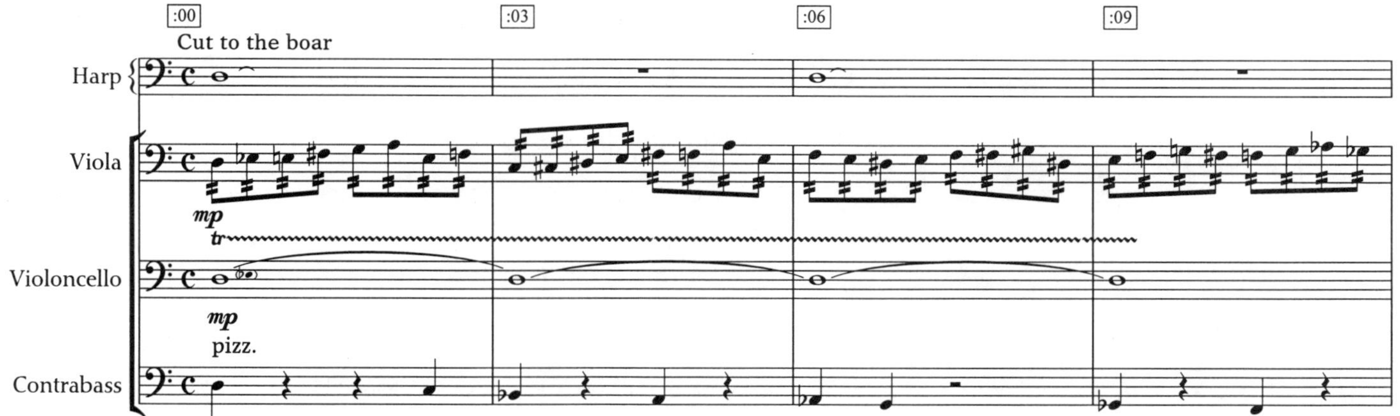

:12
a3
:15
:18
:21
2 Bs. Cl.
Bsn.
Hp.
Vln.
Va.
Vc.
Cb.
p
tr
tr
arco
p
:24
:27
:30
:33
:36
9
2 Bs. Cl.
Bsn.
Vln.
Va.
Vc.
Cb.
tr
tr
Dog attacks boar
Shade faster
Hn: brass mutes
Tpt: straight mutes
1., 3.
2.
:38
:43.5
14
3 Hn.
3 Tpt.
f
Vln.
Va.
div.
unis.
div.
unis.
div.
unis.
div.
f
sf
+ Piano R. H.
3
3
3
3
3
3
3
3
3
3
3
3
3
3
3
3
Pno.
Vc.
Cb.
+ Piano L. H. 8vb
sim.
Shade faster
hard sticks
Timp.
3

18
:49
:55.5
(1., 3.
2.)
a3, straight mutes
mf
3 Hn.
3 Tpt.
Tbn.
Tba.
unis.
div.
unis.
div.
unis.
div.
Vln.
Va.
Pno.
Vc.
Cb.
3 3 3 3 3 3 3 3 3 3 3 3 3 3 3 3 3 3
Timp.
3 3 3 3 3 3

1:01
1:06.5
22
cut to boar
Stuie cocks his rifle
A. Fl.
2 Bs. Cl.
2 Bs. Cl.
Bsn.
Bsn.
(1., 3.
2.)
3 Hn.
3 Tpt.
(a3)
1., 2.
Tbn.
Tba.
3., Tba.
Vln.
Va.
Pno.
Vc.
Cb.
mp
3 3 3 3
Timp.
3 3 3
mf

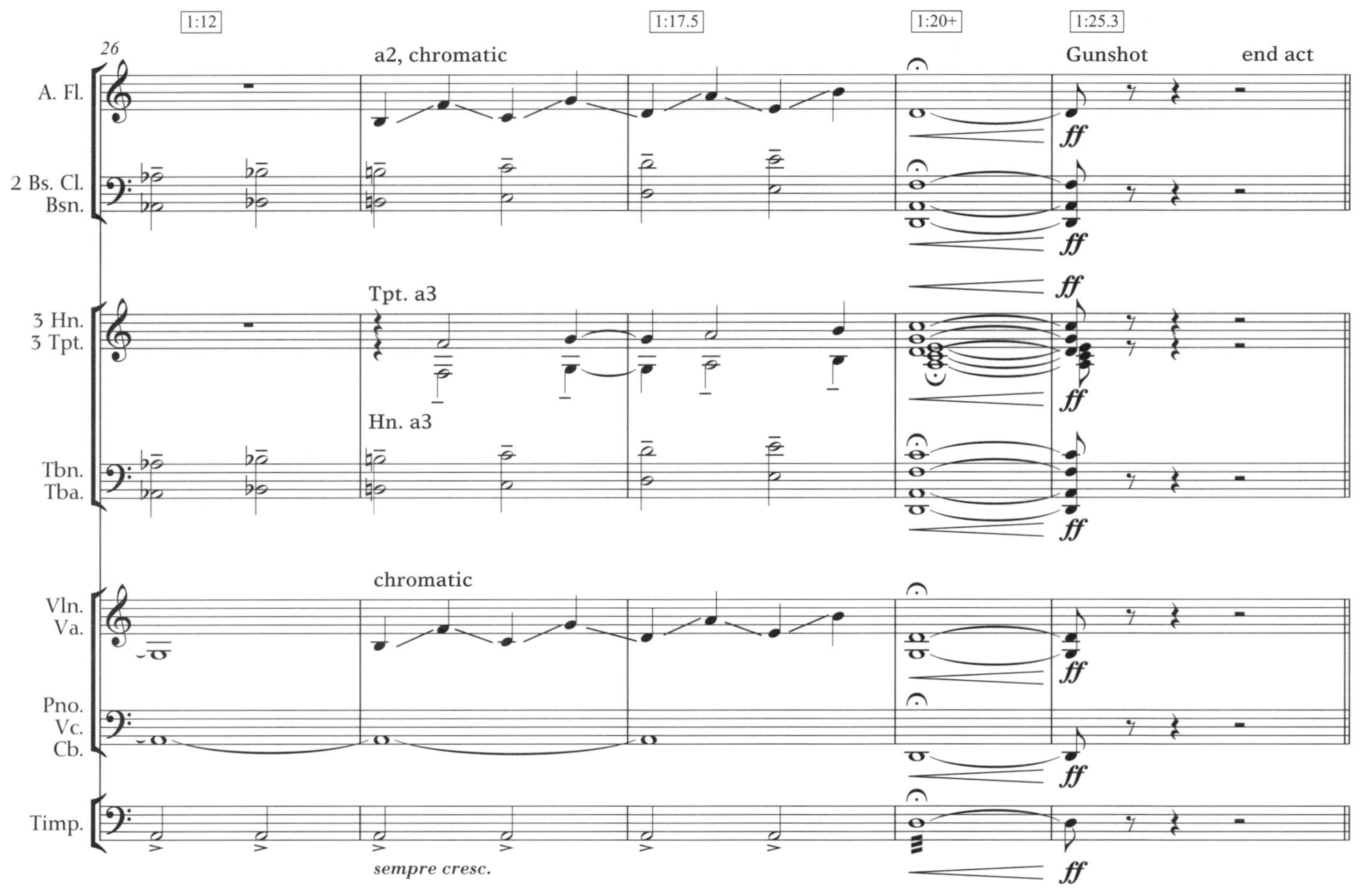

Example 4
M–16 Passion Play (Episode I)
⊙ **CD Track 4**

The dark woodwinds and the celli give us a very good indication that Mary is up to no good here. The entrance of the "Mary Carson Theme" is delayed until she makes her move toward Ralph at :10 seconds. That spot was picked because it falls between her two lines of dialogue, thus giving the theme a clear and effective entrance. The woodwinds and low strings provide a dark underpinning for the English horn solo first, and later the solo clarinet. At 1:12, things are getting a bit steamy. Soli strings take over, adding weight as Mary continues to chide him. The strings ascend slowly and then back off to a pianissimo at 1:42 creating a breathless moment as Mary is really putting the pressure on Ralph. She slowly turns to leave at 1:55.5, breaking the tension and leaving poor Father Ralph to ponder what this is all about. The celli and basses begin a line that is joined contrapuntally by the violas as we cut into the church to see Ralph agonizing over this conflict he is having between the flesh and the cloth. The full impact is reached as we cut to the crucifix at 2:48.1, when his emotion starts to subside. The cue ends as Meggie, who has entered the church during the ordeal, speaks.

Production: **THE THORNBIRDS** Production #: 167601
Cue: **M - 16 "PASSION PLAY"**
Begins at **d2:09:41:29**

ABS SMPTE #(df)	REL. TIME:		
			AFTER GETTING CAUGHT IN THE RAIN RALPH DISROBES AND DRIES HIMSELF OFF ON THE PORCH. CAMERA PANS LEFT TO MARY CARSON STANDING AT THE SCREEN DOOR WATCHING HIM.
d2:09:41:29	0:00.00		MUSIC BEGINS IN MS - MARY AT THE SCREEN DOOR WATCHING RALPH
d2:09:44:06	0:02.24	CUT	MCS - RALPH DRYING HIMSELF OFF
d2:09:48:26	0:06.91	CUT	MS - MARY WATCHING
d2:09:52.28	0:10.98		MARY: **"YOU ARE THE MOST BEAUTIFUL MAN I HAVE EVER SEEN. . ."**
d2:09:56:01	0:14.08	CUT	MS - RALPH LOOKING UP OFF STAGE **". . .RALPH DE BRICASSART."**
d2:09:57:29	0:14.95		PAUSE
d2:10:00:00	0:16.02	CUT	MS - MARY AT THE SCREEN DOOR
d2:10:00:12	0:18.05		SHE MOVES TO HER RIGHT
d2:10:02:10	0:18.45	CUT	FS - BACK ANGLE OF MARY WALKING TOWARD NUDE RALPH
d2:10:04:06	0:20.39		MARY: **"BUT OF COURSE YOU ALREADY KNOW THAT."**
d2:10:06:12	0:24.46	CUT	CS - FAVORING MARY WITH HER HANDS ON RALPH'S SHOULDERS
d2:10:08:19	0:26.69		MARY MASSAGES HIS SHOULDERS
d2:10:09:24	0:27.86		MARY: **"CURIOUS HOW YOU VIEW US MORTALS WITH CONTEMPT FOR ADMIRING THAT BEAUTY AND YET YOU REDUCE IT WITHOUT COMPUNCTION. . ."**
d2:10:21:28	0:40.01	CUT	PAUSE IN MS - FAVORING RALPH
d2:10:27:08	0:45.35		RALPH: **"I THOUGHT IT WAS MY SOUL YOU WERE AFTER MARY."**
d2:10:29:14	0:47.55	CUT	CS - FAVORING MARY: **"IT IS, BECAUSE AT MY AGE OFFICIALLY I'M SUPPOSED TO BE BEYOND THE DRIVES OF MY BODY. . .AND ONE MUSTN'T EXPECT MIRACLES. . .EVEN FROM YOU."**
d2:10:47:29	1:06.07	CUT	PAUSE IN MS - FAVORING RALPH
d2:10:50:17	1:08.67		MARY: **"HOW MANY WOMEN HAVE LOVED YOU RALPH. . .BESIDES YOUR MOTHER"**
d2:10:53:25	1:11.94		PAUSE
d2:10:56:04	1:14.24		RALPH: **"DID SHE LOVE ME. . .I DON'T KNOW. . .SHE ENDED UP HATING ME."**
d2:11:02:00	1:20.05		PAUSE
d2:11:02:11	1:20.41	CUT	CS - FAVORING MARY
d2:11:03:25	1:21.88		MARY: **"BECAUSE YOU DIDN'T NEED HER."**
d2:11:05:23	1:23.82	CUT	PAUSE IN MS - FAVORING RALPH
d2:11:07:07	1:25.29		RALPH: **"BECAUSE I NEEDED GOD MORE."**
d2:11:09:04	1:27.19	CUT	PAUSE IN CS - FAVORING MARY

d2:11:12:06	1:30.26		MARY: **"INTERESTING. . .AND NOW. . .NOW YOU CAN'T NEED ANY WOMAN CAN YOU CARDINAL DE BRICASSART?"**
d2:11:44:23	2:02.86		SHE PULLS THE DOOR TO THE HOUSE OPEN
d2:11:36:21	1:54.78	CUT	FS - MARY AND RALPH AS SHE TURNS TOWARD THE CAMERA
d2:11:38:17	1:56.65		SHE WALKS TOWARD THE CAMERA
d2:11:36:21	1:54.78	CUT	FS - MARY AND RALPH AS SHE TURNS TOWARD THE CAMERA
d2:11:38:17	1:56.65		SHE WALKS TOWARD THE CAMERA
d2:11:44:23	2:02.86		SHE PULLS THE DOOR TO THE HOUSE OPEN
d2:11:26:00	1:44.07	CUE	PAUSE IN MS - FAVORING RALPH
d2:11:27:28	1:46.01	CUT	CS - FAVORING MARY WITH HER HANDS AROUND HIS NECK
d2:11:31:14	1:49.54		SHE SLIDES HER HANDS DOWN HIS CHEST
d2:11:31:28	1:50.01	CUT	MS - FAVORING RALPH
d2:11:33:29	1:52.05	CUT	CS - FAVORING MARY
d2:11:36:15	1:54.58		SHE TURNS TO HER LEFT
d2:11:47:01	2:05.13		AND WALKS INSIDE
d2:11:48:15	2:06.59		SHE CLOSES THE DOOR
d2:11:51:03	2:09.20	CUT	MS - STATUE OF MADONNA
d2:11:56:04	2:14.23	CUT	MS - RALPH STANDING AT AN ALTAR PRAYING
d2:12:00:22	2:18.77		RALPH LOWERS HIS HEAD
d2:12:01:18	2:19.64		HE LOWERS DOWN INTO FRAME - GETTING ON HIS KNEES
d2:12:02:07	2:20.27		RALPH IS ON HIS KNEES WITH HIS FACE LEANING AGAINST HIS HANDS
d2:12:08:20	2:26.71		HE LOOKS UP AT THE ALTAR
d2:12:10:17	2:28.62	CUT	MS - HIS POV OF JESUS
d2:12:12:27	2:30.62	CUT	CS - RALPH
d2:12:17:06	2:35.26	CUT	FS - BACK ANGLE OF RALPH AT THE ALTAR
d2:12:19:10	2:37.39		BACK ANGLE OF MEGGIE WALKING INTO VIEW
d2:12:21:00	2:39.06		SHE STANDS
d2:12:22:29	2:41.03		SHE BOWS
d2:12:23:05	2:41.23	CUT	MS - FRONT ANGLE OF MEGGIE BOWING
d2:12:24:05	2:42.23		SHE CROSSES HERSELF
d2:12:28:11	2:46.43	CUT	CS - RALPH LOOKING UP AT ALTAR
d2:12:30:03	2:48.17		HE LOOKS AWAY FROM THE ALTAR
d2:12:43:14	3:01.55		RALPH RISES
d2:12:49:27	3:07.99	CUT	FS - BACK ANGLE OF MEGGIE AND RALPH
d2:12:51:20	3:09.76		RALPH TURNS TOWARD MEGGIE

d2:12:53:12	3:11.49 CUT	MS - MEGGIE	
d2:12:54:19	3:12.73	MEGGIE: **"FATHER I'M SO GLAD YOU'RE BACK. . ."** MUSIC TAILS	
		TOTAL TIME - 3:12:73	

M-16 Episode I

Passion Play

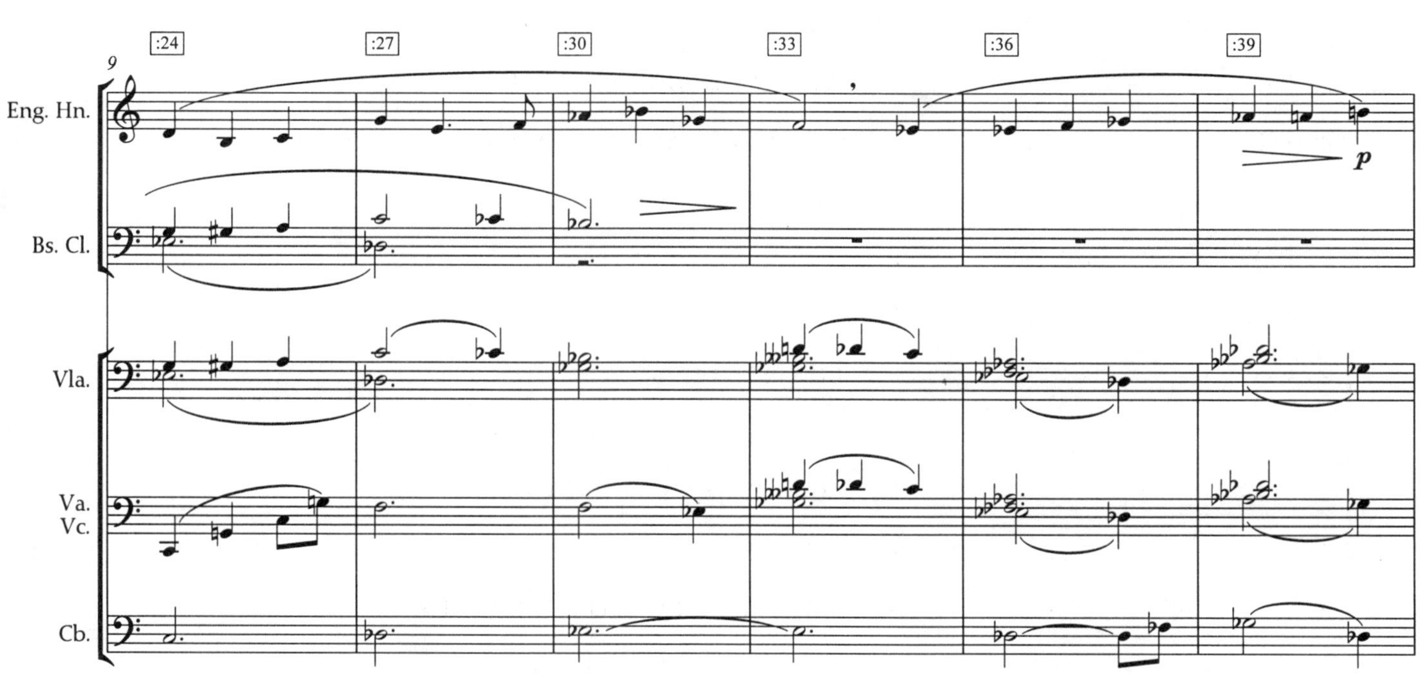

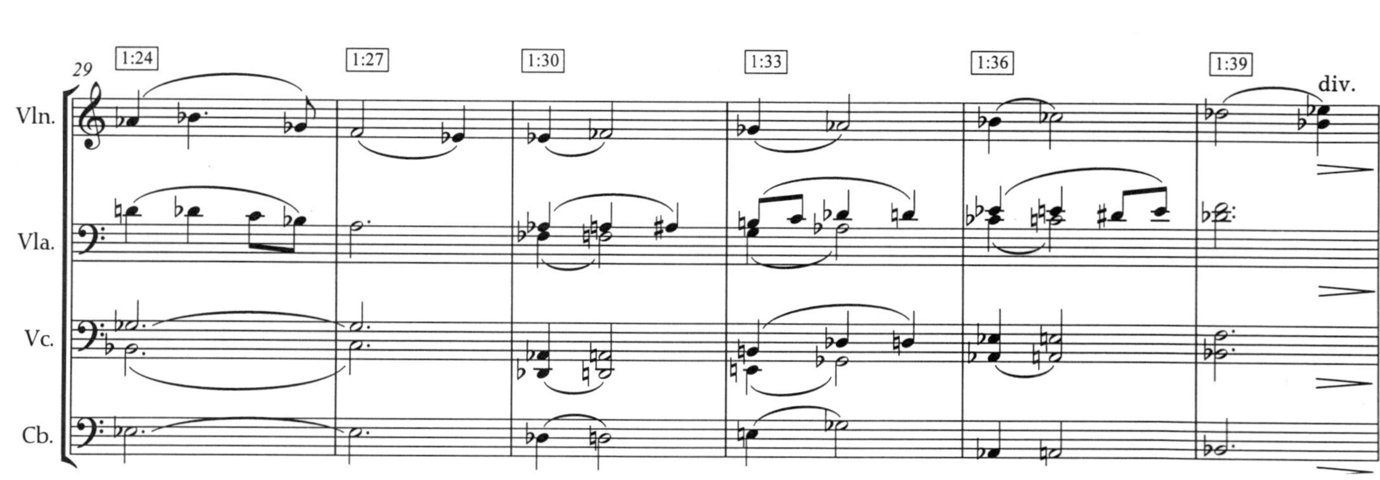

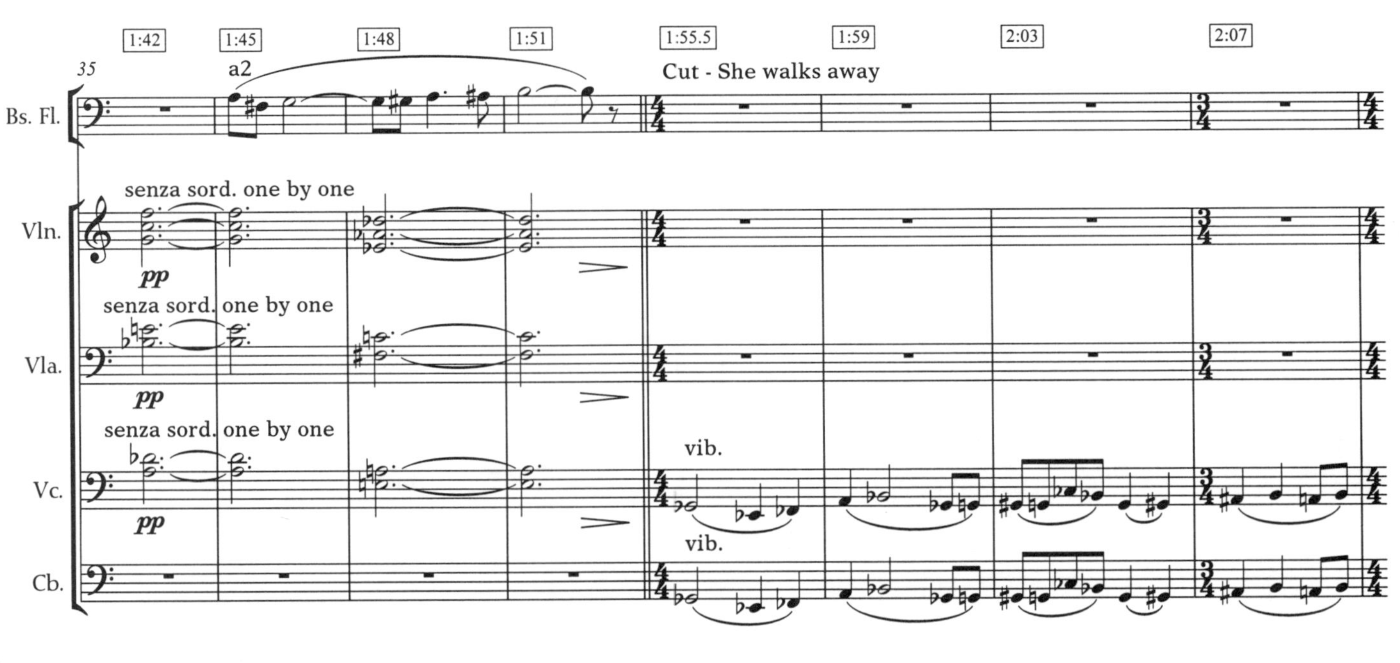
1:42
1:45
1:48
1:51
1:55.5
1:59
2:03
2:07
35
a2
Cut - She walks away
Bs. Fl.
senza sord. one by one
Vln.
pp
senza sord. one by one
Vla.
pp
senza sord. one by one
Vc.
pp
vib.
Cb.
vib.

2:09.9
2:13.5
2:17
2:20.5
2:24
2:27.5
43
chromatic
Vln.
Vla.
p, espr.
Vc.
Cb.

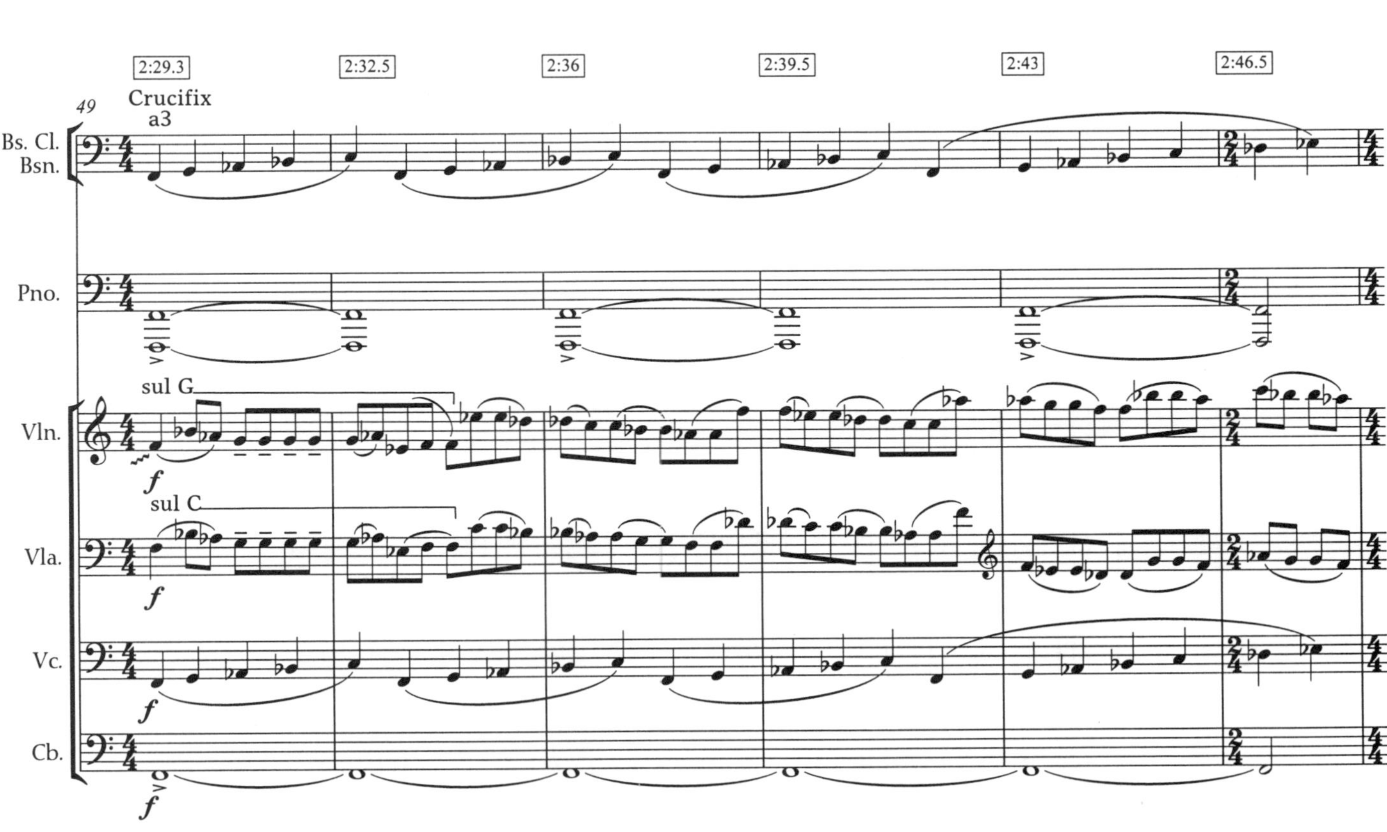
2:29.3
2:32.5
2:36
2:39.5
2:43
2:46.5
49
Crucifix
a3
2 Bs. Cl.
Bsn.
Pno.
sul G
Vln.
f
sul C
Vla.
f
Vc.
f
Cb.
f

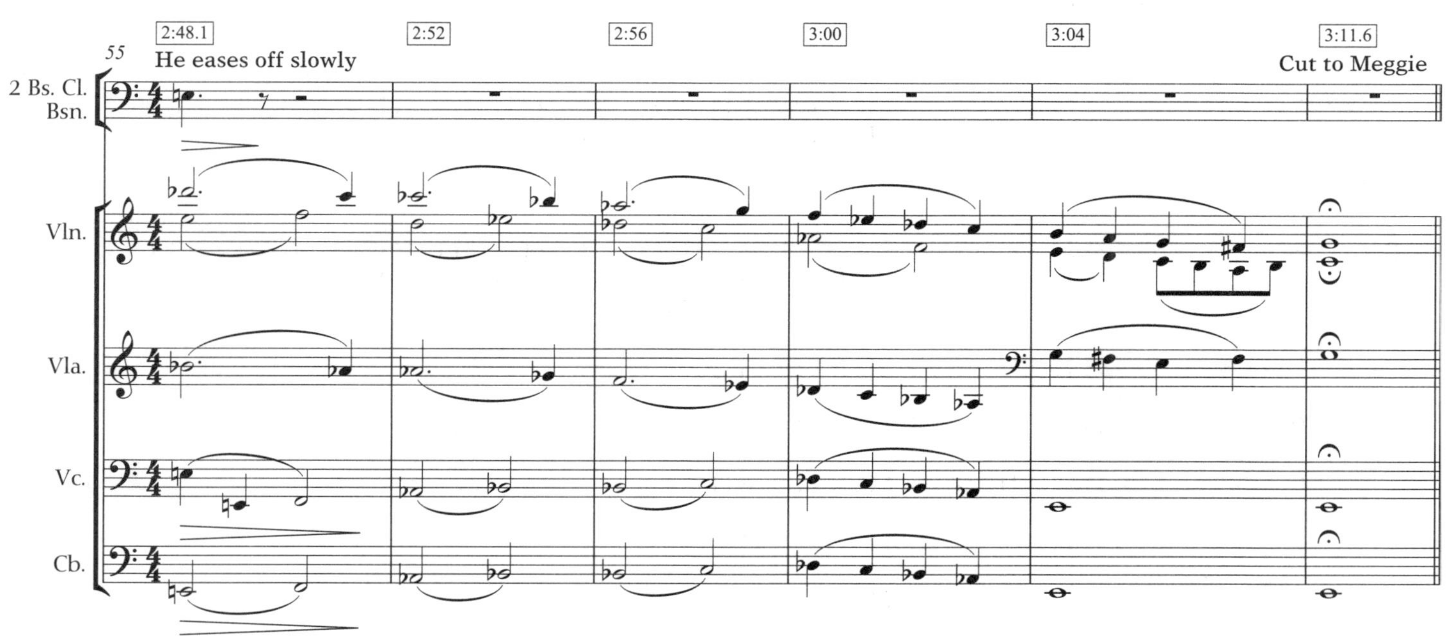

Example 5
M–21 The Story of the Thorn Bird (Episode I)
⊙ CD Track 5

This cue is a good example of writing behind a very delicate dialogue scene. The regular harp begins on a pedeal point, E – F♭ – E. This simple device is effective because it gives each note a little longer decay, thus giving an overlapping effect. The muted piano adds a softness to the overall blend.

The string divisi at :06 is a very useful one for a section of this size. The triad is covered, two on a part, by both the muted violas and celli. It's an effective voicing.

The dramatic point of this scene if Ralph's telling little Meggie The Story of The Thorn Bird. I felt this little story should have a setting all its own. It recurs in a later episode. At :39 seconds there is a pause just before he says, "There's a story." The muted piano proved to be an effective color for the theme, softer than the regular piano and not as childlikee as the celesta, the divided, muted violins form a transparent backing.

I can't stress enough to young writers the effectiveness of simplicity. In scenes of this type, think of the overall mood you wish to create. Retain the thought that "less is enough."

Production: **THE THORNBIRDS**   Production #: 167601
Cue: **M - 21 "THE STORY OF THE THORN BIRD"**
Begins at **d2:31:45:28**

ABS SMPTE #(df)	REL. TIME:		
			ACT OUT - AFTER TALKING WITH PADDY RALPH CLIMBS THE STAIRS TO MEGGIE'S BEDROOM. HE ENTERS MEGGIE'S BEDROOM AND WALKS TO HER BEDSIDE. HE SITS AND CONSOLES HER.
d2:31:45:28	0:00.00		MUSIC BEGINS IN M2S - RALPH AND MEGGIE
d2:31:47:29	0:02.04		RALPH: **"MEGGIE FRANK HAD TO LEAVE."**
d2:31:49:26	0:03.94	CUT	CS - MEGGIE
d2:31:50:11	0:04.44		MEGGIE: **"WHY?"**
d2:31:51:01	0:05.11	CUT	CS - RALPH
d2:31:51:15	0:05.57		RALPH: **"BECAUSE. . .BECAUSE IT HURT HIM TOO MUCH TO STAY."**

d2:31:56:27	0:10.98	CUT	PAUSE IN CS - MEGGIE
d2:31:58:11	0:12.45		MEGGIE: **"BUT IT'LL HURT MORE WITHOUT MOM AND ME. . .BECAUSE WE'RE THE ONES WHO LOVE HIM. . ."**
d2:32:03:11	0:17.38	CUT	PAUSE IN CS - RALPH
d2:32:06:21	0:20.72		RALPH: **"MEGGIE. . .FOR EACH OF US THERE COMES A TIME WHEN HE MUST SEARCH FOR THE THING HE THINKS HE NEEDS ABOVE ALL ELSE NO MATTER WHAT IT COSTS."**
d2:32:18:02	0:32.10	CUT	PAUSE IN CS - MEGGIE
d2:32:18:29	0:33.00		MEGGIE: **"YOU MEAN THE THING THAT'LL MAKE HIM HAPPY?"**
d2:32:20:26	0:34.90	CUT	PAUSE IN CS - RALPH
d2:32:22:03	0:36.14		RALPH: **"HAPPY."**
d2:32:22:14	0:36.50		PAUSE
d2:32:28:12	0:42.44		RALPH: **"THERE'S A STORY. . ."**
d2:32:29:13	0:43.48	CUT	MS - RALPH AND MEGGIE LOOKING AT HIM
d2:32:31:03	0:45.15		RALPH: **". . .A LEGEND. . .ABOUT A BIRD THAT SINGS JUST ONCE IN IT'S LIFE. . ."**
d2:32:36:01	0:50.08		PAUSE
d2:32:36:14	0:50.52	CUT	CS - RALPH
d2:32:37:13	0:51.48		RALPH: **"FROM THE MOMENT IT LEAVES IT'S NEST IT SEARCHES FOR A THORN TREE AND NEVER RESTS UNTIL ITS FOUND ONE AND THEN IT SINGS MORE SWEETLY THAN ANY OTHER CREATURE ON THE FACE OF THE EARTH. . .SINGING, IT IMPALES ITSELF ON THE LONGEST, SHARPEST, THORN. . ."**
d2:32:58:17	1:12.64	CUT	CS - MEGGIE
d2:32:59:00	1:13.07		RALPH: **". . .BUT AS IT DIES IT RISES ABOVE IT'S OWN AGONY. . ."**
d2:33:06:08	1:20.28	CUT	CS - RALPH: **". . .TO OUTSING THE LARK AND THE NIGHTENGALE, THE THORN BIRD PAYS ITS LIFE FOR JUST ONE SONG BUT THE WHOLE WORLD STILLS TO LISTEN AND GOD IN HIS HEAVEN. . .SMILES. . .**
d2:33:32:07	1:46.27		PAUSE
d2:33:32:19	1:46.67	CUT	CS - FAVORING MEGGIE
d2:33:37:00	1:51.04		MEGGIE: **"WHAT DOES IT MEAN FATHER?"**
d2:33:38:07	1:52.28		PAUSE
d2:33:38:18	1:52.65	CUT	CS - RALPH
d2:33:39:29	1:54.01		MEGGIE MOVES TOWARD RALPH
d2:33:41:11	1:55.42		HE EMBRACES HER
d2:33:44:03	1:58.15		RALPH: **"THAT THE BEST IS BOUGHT ONLY AT THE COST OF GREAT. . .PAIN."**
d2:33:52:23	2:06.83	CUT	PAUSE IN CS - MEGGIE
d2:33:57:00	2:11.06		START FADE OUT
d2:33:57:24	2:11.87		MUSIC FULL OUT TO BLACK AND END OF ACT
			TOTAL TIME - 2:11.87

The Story of the Thorn Bird

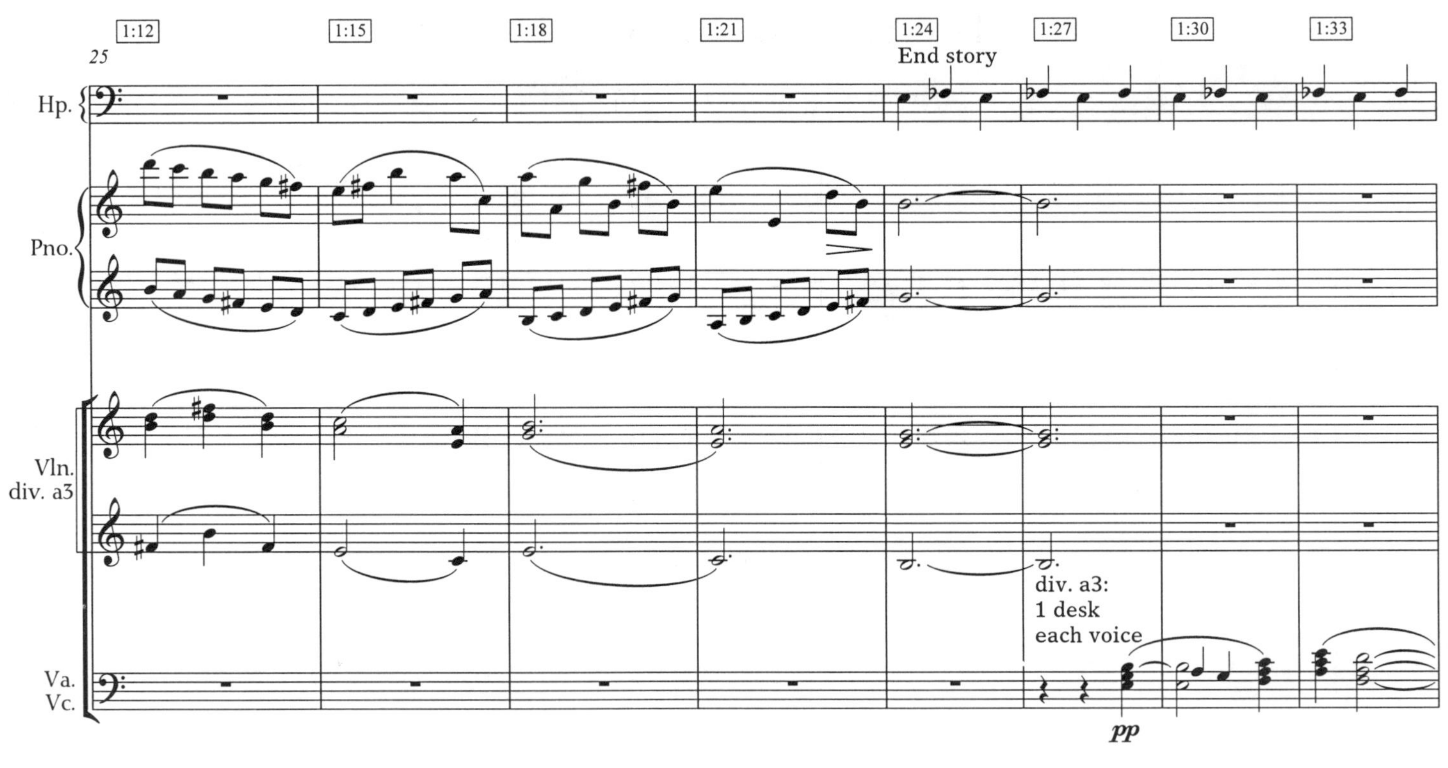
1:12
1:15
1:18
1:21
1:24
1:27
1:30
1:33
End story
25
Hp.
Pno.
Vln.
div. a3
Va.
Vc.
div. a3:
1 desk
each voice
pp

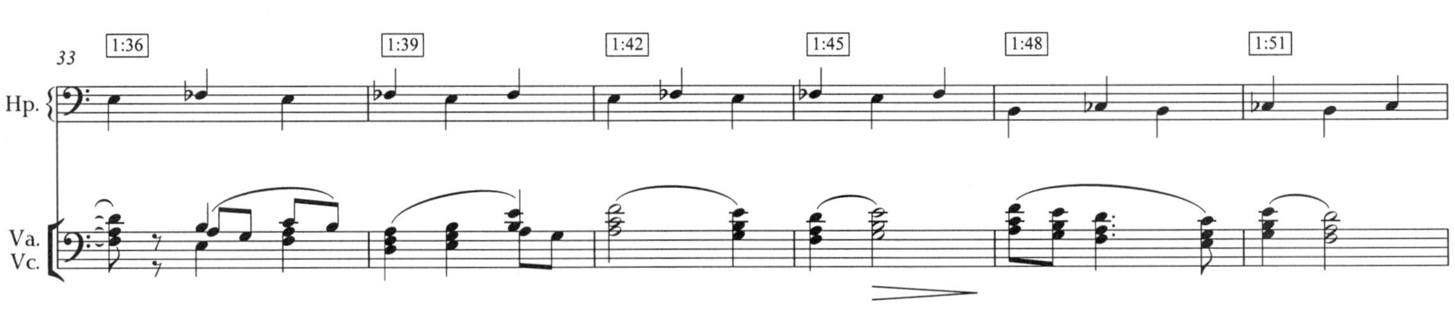
1:36
1:39
1:42
1:45
1:48
1:51
33
Hp.
Va.
Vc.

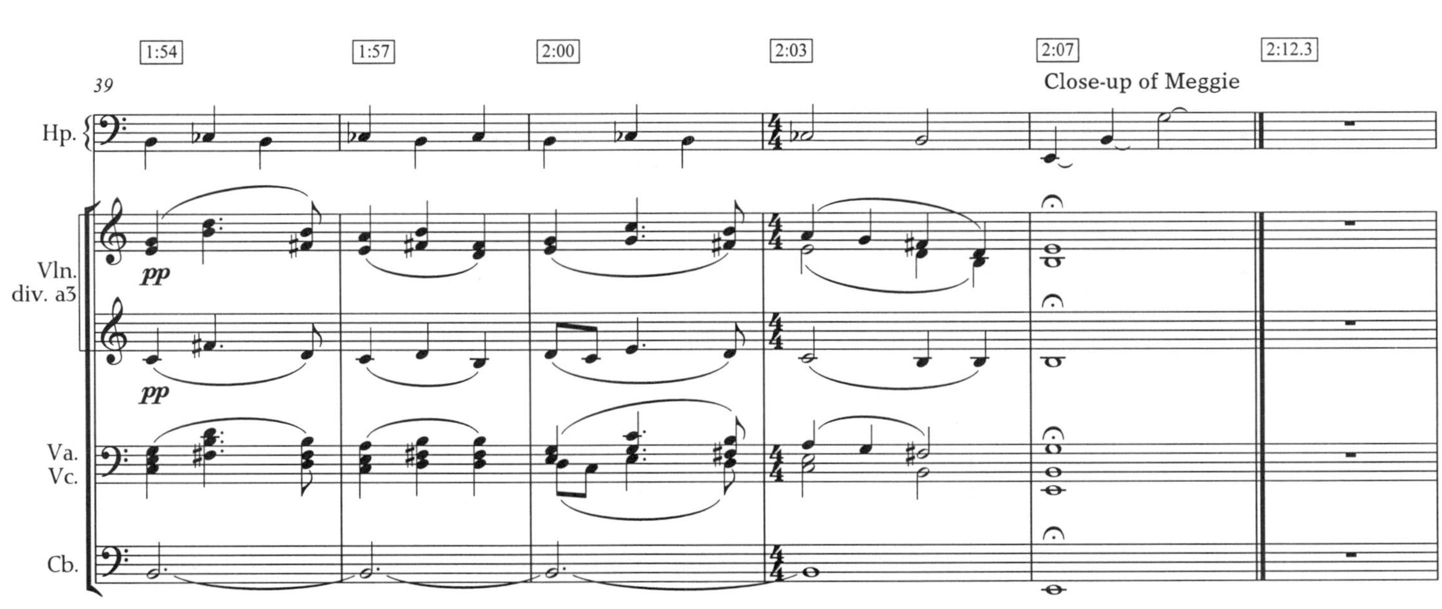
1:54
1:57
2:00
2:03
2:07
2:12.3
Close-up of Meggie
39
Hp.
Vln.
div. a3
pp
pp
Va.
Vc.
Cb.

Example 6
M–30 Grown Up Meggie (Episode I)
⊙ **CD Track 6**

Here we have our first look at "grown-up Meggie." Director Daryl Duke makes a moving event of her entrance to the party. Everyone at the party, especially Ralph, is stunned by her beauty.

Since the scene is a visual experience, the music could take over completely. The muted piano, regular harp and song bells lead to a full string treatment of "Meggie's Theme." At :25 seconds the rolling eighth note figure which we introduced in the high register in M-7 ("Awestruck Meggie"), is now given to the woodwinds, muted piano and harp in a much lower register.

Throughout the piece, until the last four bars, the basses, playing pizzicato, keep the "waltz" feeling alive. There is enough movement in the orchestra to negate the need for any other rhythm instruments.

Production: **THE THORNBIRDS**   Production #: 167601
Cue: **M - 30 "GROWN UP MEGGIE"**
Begins at **d3:10:20:16**

ABS SMPTE #(df)	REL. TIME:		
			WE ARE AT THE HOUSE FOR MARY'S BIRTHDAY PARTY. ONE OF THE GUESTS LOOKS UP ASKING: "WHO IS THAT?"
d3:10:20:16	0:00.00	CUT	MUSIC BEGINS IN FS - MEGGIE DESCENDING THE STAIRS
d3:10:24:14	0:03.94	CUT	M2S - PADDY AND FIONA
d3:10:27:01	0:06.51		FS - MEGGIE DESCENDING THE STAIRS
d3:10:28:05	0:07.64		SHE PAUSES ON THE STAIRS WITH A MONA LISA GRIN
d3:10:29:06	0:08.68	CUT	CAMERA PANNING LEFT IN MS - PARTY GUEST LOOKING UP AT HER
d3:10:29:17	0:09.04		CAMERA REVEALS RALPH
d3:10:29:27	0:09.38		RALPHS LOOKS UP OFF STAGE AT MEGGIE
d3:10:32:02	0:11.54		CAMERA HOLDS IN MS - RALPH
d3:10:34:11	0:13.85		RALPHS WALKS TOWARD THE CAMERA
d3:10:37:21	0:17.18		HE STANDS
d3:10:38:26	0:18.35	CUT	MS - MEGGIE SLOWLY DESCENDING THE STAIRS
d3:10:41:06	0:20.69		CAMERA FOLLOWS HER AS SHE SPEEDS UP DESCENDING THE STAIRS
d3:10:43:15	0:22.99		STANDS ON THE BOTTOM STEP AS SHE SHAKES HANDS WITH A LADY GUEST
d3:10:44:23	0:24.26		SHE SHAKES HANDS WITH ANOTHER LADY GUEST
d3:10:45:15	0:24.99		SHE TURNS HER HEAD TOWARD THE CAMERA
d3:10:45:19	0:25.13		SHE LOOKS OFFSTAGE
d3:10:46:13	0:25.93		SHE LOOKS DOWN AT THE LADY GUESTS
d3:10:48:01	0:27.53		SHE WALKS OFF THE BOTTOM STEP BETWEEN THE TWO LADY GUESTS
d3:10:49:24	0:29.30		SHE SHAKES HANDS WITH ANOTHER LADY GUEST
d3:10:50:11	0:29.86		SHE LOOKS OFFSTAGE TOWARD THE CAMERA

d3:10:56:05	0:35.67		PAUSE AS SHE LOOKS AT HIM
d3:10:57:01	0:36.54		PARTY GUEST STANDING IN FRONT OF HER: **"YOU'RE SO BEAUTIFUL."**
d3:10:55:05	0:34.67		PAUSE AS HE WALKS AWAY
d3:10:55:18	0:35.10	CUT	MS - MEGGIE LOOKING AT RALPH SMILING
d3:10:55:29	0:35.47		PARTY GUEST WALKING INTO FRAME: **"MEGGIE."**
d3:10:50:29	0:30.46	CUT	MS - RALPH LOOKING AT MEGGIE
d3:10:54:05	0:33.67		HE TURNS TOWARD TWO LADY GUESTS WITH WHOM HE'S STANDING
d3:10:54:12	0:33.90		RALPH: **"EXCUSE ME."**
d3:10:57:29	0:37.47		PAUSE
d3:10:58:06	0:37.70		MEGGIE: **"OH THANKS. . ."**
d3:10:59:05	0:38.67		PAUSE
d3:11:00:23	0:40.21		HE WALKS OFF
d3:11:01:29	0:41.41		MEGGIE WALKS TOWARD RALPH
d3:11:03:10	0:42.78	CUT	MS - RALPH STEPPING INTO VIEW LOOKING AT HER
d3:11:04:12	0:43.84		HE LOOKS AT ANOTHER PARTY GUEST
d3:11:04:25	0:44.28		AND TALKS WITH HER
d3:11:05:20	0:45.11	CUT	MS - MEGGIE SLOWLY STEPPING FORWARD LOOKING OFFSTAGE AT RALPH
d3:11:06:28	0:46.38		SHE LOOKS DOWN
d3:11:08:24	0:48.25		SHE STANDS LOOKING UP TOWARD HIM
d3:11:11:21	0:51.15	CUT	MS - RALPH TALKING WITH LADY GUEST
d3:11:12:15	0:51.95		HE LOOKS OFFSTAGE AT MEGGIE
d3:11:15:29	0:55.42	CUT	MS - MEGGIE LOOKING AT HIM
d3:11:17:24	0:57.26		SHE SMILES. . .
d3:11:18:25	0:58.29		LOOKS DOWN AND SLOWLY WALKS
d3:11:19:18	0:59.06	CUT	MS - RALPH BEING POLITE LISTENING AND TALKING WITH THE PARTY GUEST
d3:11:22:24	1:02.26		RALPH LOOKS OFF STAGE AT MEGGIE
d3:11:24:05	1:03.63	CUT	MSC - MEGGIE
d3:11:24:19	1:04.10		SHE LOOKS OFFSTAGE AT RALPH
d3:11:28:16	1:08.00	CUT	MS - RALPH
d3:11:30:18	1:10.07		FEELING UNCOMFORTABLE HE LOOKS AROUND
d3:11:33:20	1:13.14		A GUEST PUTS HIS HAND ON RALPH'S SHOULDER AS RALPH TURNS TOWARD GUEST
d3:11:38:19	1:18.11		RALPH LOOKS AWAY FROM MEGGIE
d3:11:40:03	1:19.58		HE'S LEAD AWAY STILL LOOKING OFF STAGE
d3:11:41:19	1:21.11		RALPH LOOKS AWAY FROM MEGGIE

d3:11:44:24	1:24.28	CUT	MS - MEGGIE LOOKING OFF STAGE TOWARD RALPH
d3:11:47:25	1:27.32		SHE LOOKS DOWN
d3:11:48:10	1:27.82		SHE LOOKS UP IN RALPH'S DIRECTION
d3:11:50:29	1:30.46		SHE STARES
d3:11:53:04	1:32.63	CUT	FS - THE PARTY AND MUSIC IS OUT
			TOTAL TIME - 1:32.63

M-30
HENRY MANCINI
Cl BSN
B.C.
B.C.
Cl BSN

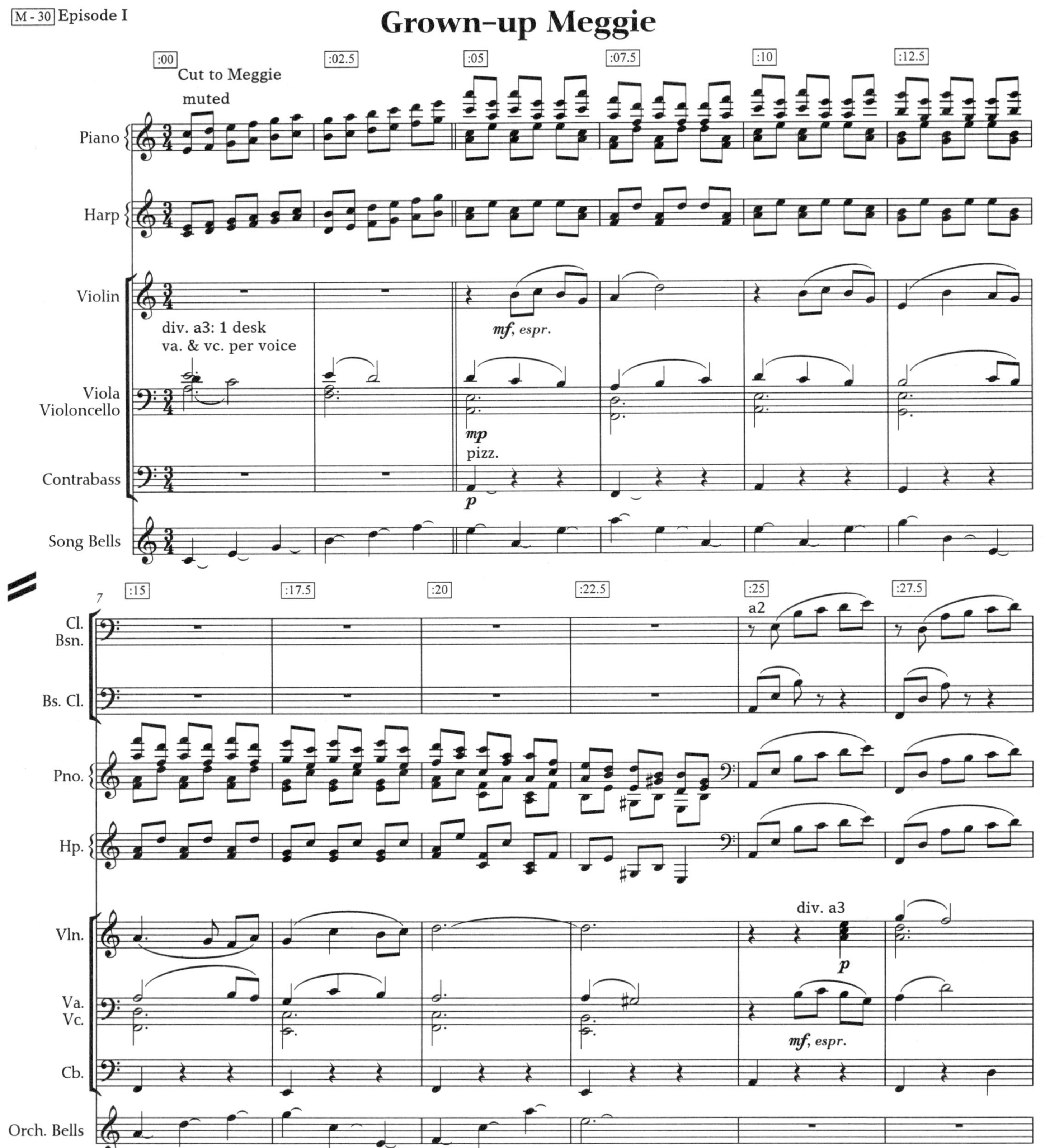
M - 30 Episode I
Grown-up Meggie
Cut to Meggie
muted
Piano
Harp
Violin
div. a3: 1 desk
va. & vc. per voice
mf, espr.
Viola
Violoncello
mp
pizz.
Contrabass
p
Song Bells
:00
:02.5
:05
:07.5
:10
:12.5
Cl.
Bsn.
a2
Bs. Cl.
Pno.
Hp.
Vln.
div. a3
p
Va.
Vc.
mf, espr.
Cb.
Orch. Bells
:15
:17.5
:20
:22.5
:25
:27.5

Cl.
Bsn.
Bs. Cl.
Pno.
Hp.
Vln.
Va.
Vc.
Cb.
13
:30
(a2)
:32.5
:35
:37.5
a2
:40
a2
:42.5
a2
Soli
div.
19
:45
mf
mf
:47.5
:50
:52.5
:55
:57.5
1:00
Fl.
Pno.
Vln.
Va.
Vc.
Cb.
26
1:02.5
1:05
Solo
mf
1:07.5
1:10
1:12.5
1:15
+ Hp.
(muted)
p
Ped.
Ped.
Ped.
Ped.
Solo
mf
(Gli altri)
pp

Example 7
M–40 Ralph Leaves Meggie (Episode I)
⊙ CD Track 7

This is the last scene in Episode I. Starting quietly enough, the scenes move to an emotionally charged fadeout. The cue, of course, called for "Meggie's Theme" again. The theme is interpolated by a solo muted violin and solo muted viola, doubled an octave lower. The muted piano forms the harmonic background.   Note the use of the pedal which sustains the harmony over the bar over each chord change.

At :28.6 seconds things start to heat up. The rolling eighth note figures, now in the low strings, harp and muted piano lead us into the violins playing the theme, backed by three French horns providing the harmony.

Frustrated, Ralph drives off leaving Meggie standing alone as the camera pulls back from her to a very long shot of Drogheda, ending the episode.

I saved my low brass for the pull–back at 1:28.7. The trumpets enter at 1:40 1/2 for the tutti finale.

Production: **THE THORNBIRDS**   Production #: 167601
Cue: **M - 40 "RALPH LEAVES MEGGIE"**

ABS SMPTE #(df)	REL. TIME:		
			IN THE FINAL SCENE, RALPH IS TALKING TO MEGGIE. SHE BEGS HIM: "YOU CAN MARRY ME. YOU LOVE ME!" RALPH COUNTERS WITH: "BUT I LOVE GOD MORE!"
	0:00.0		START MUSIC WELL INTO THE CUT TO MEGGIE AS HE TAKES HIS HAND AWAY FROM HER CHIN
	0:01.1		SHE LOOKS DOWN
	0:02.5	CUT	RALPH
	0:04.8		HE SAYS WITH A SHAKING VOICE: **"I DO LOVE YOU, MEGGIE. I ALWAYS WILL. BUT I CAN'T BE A HUSBAND TO YOU."**

0:12.3	CUT	PAUSE. MEGGIE. . .
0:12.8		. . .AS SHE LOOKS UP AT HIM
0:13.9	CUT	RALPH
0:14.5		RALPH: **"IF ONLY I COULD MAKE YOU UNDERSTAND WHAT BEING A PRIEST MEANS TO ME. HOW GOD. . .FILLS A NEED IN ME THAT NO HUMAN BEING EVER COULD."**
0:24.6	CUT	MEGGIE
0:25.2		MEGGIE: **"NOT EVEN ME?"**
0:26.4	CUT	PAUSE. RALPH REACTING TO HER QUESTION
0:28.6	CUT	MEGGIE AS SHE STARTS TO LEAN FORWARD TO KISS HIM
0:29.9	CUT	M2S. . .
0:30.5		. . .AS SHE KISSES HIM
0:34.7		SHE AROUSES HIM TO THE POINT WHERE HE NOW BECOMES RESPONSIVE AND THEIR KISSING BECOMES PASSIONATE
0:36.4		HE STANDS NOW AND PRESSES HER LIPS TIGHTLY TO HIS OWN
0:43.3		THE KISSING ENDS AS HE STARTS TO PUSH HER AWAY FROM HIM. HE SAYS: **"I CAN'T. I CAN'T! GOODBYE, MY MEGGIE!"**
0:49.5		EOL, AS HE LEAVES HER QUICKLY
0:51.3	CUT	RALPH HURRYING TOWARD THE FRONT GATE
0:53.5	CUT	MEGGIE
0:54.0		SHE STARTS TO GET UP TO HURRY TO THE GATE AS SHE SAYS: **"FATHER'**
0:55.6		HE STOPS AND TURNS TO LOOK BACK AT HER
0:56.9		HE STARTS TO HURRY ON OUT AGAIN, AS SHE RUNS TO THE GATE
1:00.6		SHE STOPS AT THE GATE AND CALLS OUT: **"FATHER!"**
1:01.6		EOL
1:01.9	CUT	HER POV: RALPH STARTING TO GET INTO HIS CAR
1:06.6	CUT	MCU OF MEGGIE WATCHING AT THE GATE, AS WE HEAR RALPH'S CAR START
1:08.5	CUT	HER POV: RALPH IN HIS CAR AS HE STARTS TO DRIVE OFF
1:11.9		SHE CALLS AFTER HIM: **"GO ON, THEN! GO ON TO THAT GOD OF YOURS!"**
1:15.2		PAUSE
1:17.0	CUT	MCU OF MEGGIE STANDING AT THE GATE WITH A VERY CONFIDENT LOOK ON HER FACE
1:17.8		SHE SAYS, SOFTER NOW, TO HERSELF: **"BUT YOU'LL COME BACK TO ME. . ."**
1:19.2		PAUSE
1:21.2		MEGGIE: **". . .BECAUSE I'M THE ONE WHO LOVES YOU."**
1:23.2	CUT	EOL. HER POV: RALPH'S CAR DISAPPEARING DOWN THE ROAD IN A CLOUD OF DUST

1:26.7	CUT	MEGGIE: STANDING AT THE GATE AS CAMERA STARTS TO SWEEP BACK DRAMATICALLY
1:35.1		. . .AND WE NOW SEE DROGHEDA ALSO
1:40.7		CAMERA HOLDS IN A FULL SHOT OF THE HOUSE AND GARDEN, AS SHE CONTINUES TO STAND AT THE GATE, LOOKING AFTER RALPH
1:49.2		END MUSIC IN CUT TO BLACK (COMMERCIAL) (1/2 SECOND BEFORE FULL OUT.)

M-40 Episode I

Ralph Leaves Meggie

Bs. Cl.
Bsn.
Hp.
Pno.
:53.5
:56
:58.5
1:01
Bs. Cl., Bsn. tacet
mp
Hn.
Vln.
(unis.)
Va.
Vc.
Cb.
1:08.5
1:11
1:15.5
1:19
1:22.5
Ob.
Solo
p
Vln.
div.
Va.
div.
Vc.
Cb.
mp
1:26.7
1:30
1:33.5
1:37
2 Fl.
a2
mf
Eng. Hn.
Cl.
Bsn.
Bs. Cl.
Eng. Hn., Cl.
cresc.
Hn.
Bsn., Bs. Cl.
a3
3 Tbn.
Tba.
Vln.
mf, espr.
cresc.
Va.
Vc.
Cb.
Timp.
Hp.
mf

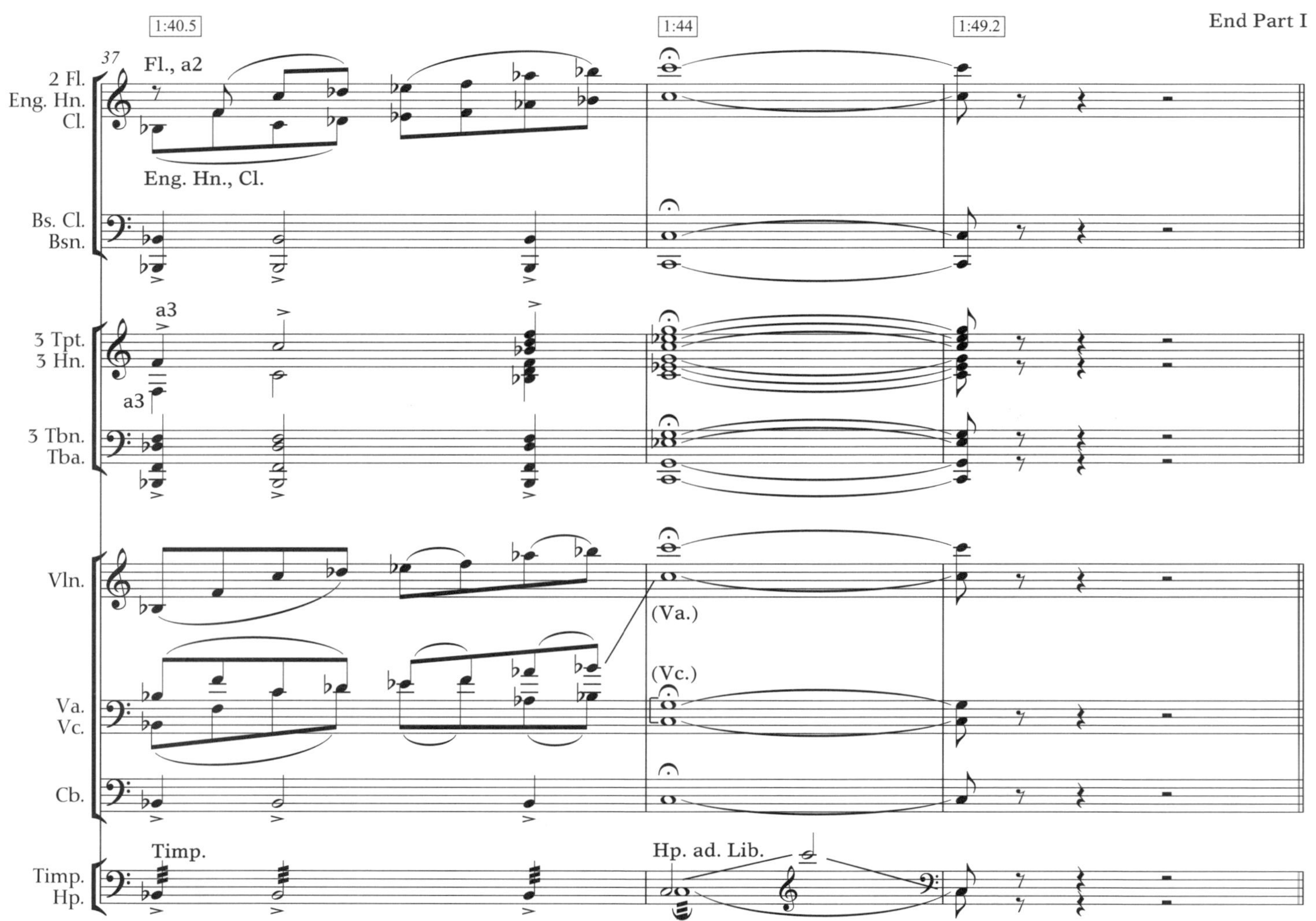

Example 8
M–1 Opening (Episode II)
⊙ CD Track 8

The opening with its long shot of Sydney harbor needed some sort of a musical statement. The problem was that the scene was very short. Had it occurred in the body of the show, I would have opted to having it covered by harbor sounds without music. Another consideration was that it sequed into the track we had made with the organ and boys' choir ("Panis Angelicus").

The incoming track was in the key of "F." I established this key in the third bar, well ahead of the organ entrance. The orchestra and the organ overlapped. In dubbing later the orchestra was faded as the organ fades in.

Production: **THE THORNBIRDS**　　Production #: 167602
Cue: **M - 1 "OPENING"**

ABS SMPTE #(df)	REL. TIME:		
	0:00.0		START MUSIC ON OPENING OF SHOW. THIS IS A FADE-IN TO A VERY LONG ESTABLISHING SHOT OF SYDNEY, AUSTRALIA. EPISODE TITLES ARE SUPERED OVER
	0:11.8		MUSIC SEGUES WITH THE ORGAN (M-2) WHICH WE HEAR COMING FROM THE CHURCH
	0:13.2	CUT	THE ESTABLISHING SHOT OF THE CHURCH
	0:20.5	CUT	THE INTERIOR

Opening (Episode 2)

Example 9
M-7 Fire on Drogheda (Episode II)
⊙ **CD Track 9**

What all epics seem to have in common is a big fire scene. This was it!

The action called for a brisk tempo – 4 clicks in :02 seconds. In examining the scene I looked for places that would give me a chance to shift gears, so to speak. These are the check points along the way that enable you to give shape and variety to the music. Incidentally, this is one of the "set" pieces I spoke of earlier. It has no relationship to any of the other thematic material in the film.

Our first check point, after a somewhat subdued opening, is at :30 seconds. This is a dissolve to the bucket brigade. At :50.6 seconds the horse–drawn fire-wagon is racing toward the fire. A definite change was needed here. At 1:23 I ducked down to get under the dialogue. At 1:53 we cut to an out–back location, where Paddy is riding through the fire. His horse starts to read at 2:11 as lightning strikes a big tree in front of him. The tree starts to fall on Paddy at 2:13.5 and he is engulfed in flames at 2:18.5. The music then builds, starting on the dissolve to an overview of the fire at 2:23. Music goes out on the cut-back to the fire at the main house. At this point the roar of the fire at its worst takes over along with the voices of people shouting and animals crying out.

Production: **THE THORNBIRDS** Production #: 167602
Cue: **M - 1 "OPENING"**

ABS SMPTE #(df)	REL. TIME:		
			FIRE HAS BROKEN OUT AT DROGHEDA AND EVERYONE PITCHES IN TO TRY TO PUT IT OUT. PADDY IS OUT ROUNDING UP THE STRAGGLER SHEEP, AS THE DRY GRASS BURNS AROUND HIM.
	0:00.0		START MUSIC ON CUT TO MLS OF THE WOMAN DRIVING A SMALL HERD OF SHEEP DOWN THE ROADWAY
	0:03.6	CUT	MEGGIE LEADING A HORSE OUT OF THE BARN
	0:06.5		SHE HOLDS THE HORSE AS A RANCHHAND COMES UP. . .
	0:09.9		. . .AND MOUNTS THE HORSE AND RIDES HIM OFF
	0:13.1		SHE STARTS TO CLOSE THE GATE AGAIN
	0:14.1		SHE PAUSES, AS SHE SEES SOMETHING OFF-CAMERA
	0:14.5	CUT	HER POV: THE FIRE BURNING VERY CLOSE TO THE HOUSE
	0:17.3	CUT	MEGGIE, AS SHE MOVES FORWARD, STARING AT THE HOUSE
	0:21.0		THE WOMEN CONTINUE LEADING THE SHEEP INTO THE SHED BEHIND HER
	0:22.8		SHE STOPS WALKING AND STARES AT THE FIRE
	0:23.8	CUT	HER POV: THE FIRE BURNING STILL CLOSER TO THE OLD HOUSE
	0:29.3		CENTER OS DISS. TO A SLIGHT TIME LAPSE. WE SEE PETE MANNING THE PUMP, AS THE WOMEN CARRY BUCKETS OF WATER AND THROW THEM ONTO THE FIRE, WHICH HAS JUST STARTED BURNING THE HOUSE
	0:36.8		MEGGIES SCOOPS UP A BUCKETFUL OF WATER. . .
	0:37.9		. . .AND HURRIES TOWARD THE HOUSE WITH IT
	0:40.9		FIONA DOES LIKEWISE
	0:47.7		SHE THROWS HER BUCKETFUL OF WATER ON THE HOUSE AS DO THE OTHER WOMEN
	0:50.3		FIONA STARTS TO RUN BACK TOWARD THE TROUGH AGAIN
	0:50.6	CUT	(SLIGHT CHANGE OF LOCATION): A CRUDE FIRE WAGON WITH SEVERAL MEN ON IT BEING PULLED BY A TEAM OF HORSES
	0:58.1	CUT	THE SMALL BRIDGE AS THE FIRE WAGON APPROACHES IT
	1:00.9		THEY START ACROSS THE BRIDGE AS THE DRIVER URGES ON THE HORSES
	1:02.7	CUT	CLOSER SHOT OF THE MEN ON THE FIREWAGON AS THEY RACE TOWARD THE BURNING HOUSE
	1:05.3	CUT	LOW-ANGLE SHOT AS THEY RIDE ACROSS THE BRIDGE
	1:09.9		THEY START INTO THE BARNYARD AND CONTINUE TOWARD THE FIRE
	1:19.1	CUT	THE BARKING DOGS IN THE PEN AS BOB RIDES UP ON HORSEBACK TOWARD THEM
	1:21.1		HE DISMOUNTS QUICKLY

1:22.5		HE YELLS TO ONE OF THE RANCHMEN: <u>**"CHARLIE, LOOSE THESE DOGS! NOW GET THAT HOSE AND BRING IT DOWN HERE. NOW YOU, YOU COME WITH ME."**</u>
1:27.3		PAUSE, AS HE GRABS ONE OF THE MEN BY THE SHOULDER AND PULLS HIM ALONG WITH HIM
1:28.1		HE STOPS BESIDE MEGGIE ON THE BUCKET BRIGADE AND SAYS: <u>**"MEGGIE, ARE YOU ALL RIGHT?"**</u>
1:29.2		MEGGIE: <u>**"YES."**</u>
1:29.5		FIONA: <u>**"TED, DID PADDY COME IN WITH YOU?"**</u>
1:30.8		TED: <u>**"NO, I HAVEN'T SEEN HIM, MRS. CLEARY."**</u>
1:32.6		MEGGIE: <u>**"JOHNNY, WHERE'S DADDY?"**</u>
1:34.6		FIONA: <u>**"HE'S UP ON THE RANGE."**</u>
1:36.3		MEGGIE: <u>**"MAYBE WE COULD CALL TO SEE IF HE CAME IN ANYWHERE?"**</u>
1:38.5		FIONA: <u>**"NO, THE LINES ARE DOWN."**</u>
1:40.0		EOL, AS THEY CONTINUE TO PASS THE BUCKETS OF WATER FRANTICALLY
1:42.6		CAMERA STARTS TO PAN OVER TO ANOTHER CORNER OF THE HOUSE
1:46.5		WE SEE MRS. SMITH COME RUNNING AROUND THE CORNER OF THE HOUSE, AS A BIG CLOUD OF BLACK SMOKE RISES BEHIND HER
1:47.1		SHE YELLS OUT: <u>**"OVER HERE!"**</u>
1:48.6		EOL, AS A COUPLE OF MEN START TO RUN IN THAT DIRECTION
1:52.2	CUT	(CHANGE OF LOCATION): THE BURNING TREES AND UNDERBRUSH OUT ON THE RANGE, AS CAMERA PANS DOWN AND AROUND IT
1:57.1	CUT	PADDY RIDING DOWN THE ROADWAY ON HIS HORSE
2:01.3	CUT	THE SKY, AS IT LIGHTS UP WITH FLASHES OF LIGHTNING AND CRACKS OF THUNDER
2:02.1	CUT	PADDY RIDING DOWN THE ROADWAY
2:07.2	CUT	THE SKY, AS BEFORE: FLASHES OF LIGHTNING AND HEAVY THUNDER. ONE PARTICULAR LIGHTNING FLASH STRIKES THE GROUND
2:08.1		WE SEE IT STRIKE A TREE, CAUSING IT TO BURST INTO FLAMES INSTANTLY
2:10.0	CUT	PADDY'S HORSE, AS IT REARS UP ON ITS HIND LEGS. . .
2:12.0		. . .CAUSING PADDY TO FALL TO THE GROUND
2:13.5	CUT	THE BURNING TREE AS IT STARTS TO FALL IN HIS DIRECTION
2:15.1	CUT	PADDY ON THE GROUND, AS HE STARTS TO TURN HIS HEAD TO LOOK UP AT IT
2:16.3		HE REACTS TO WHAT HE SEES AND SHOUTS: <u>**"NO, GOD! PLEASE!"**</u>
2:17.4	CUT	THE BURNING TREE FALLING AS HE SCREAMS
2:18.3	CUT	PADDY ON THE GROUND. . .
2:18.8		. . .AS THE BURNING TREE FALLS ON HIM, AND HE'S ENGULFED IN THE CONFLAGRATION

2:23.7		CENTER OF DISS. TO A VLS OF THE SILHOUETTE OF THE LINE OF HILLS, AS WE SEE THE ENTIRE LENGTH OF IT ENGULFED IN FLAMES
2:28.6	CUT	CLOSER SHOT OF THE BRUSH BURNING. CAMERA PANS SLOWLY
2:37.8	CUT	END MUSIC TO MS OF THE PEOPLE BACK AT THE WELL SCOOPING UP BUCKETS OF WATER FROM THE TROUGH AS A MAN PUMPS THE WATER

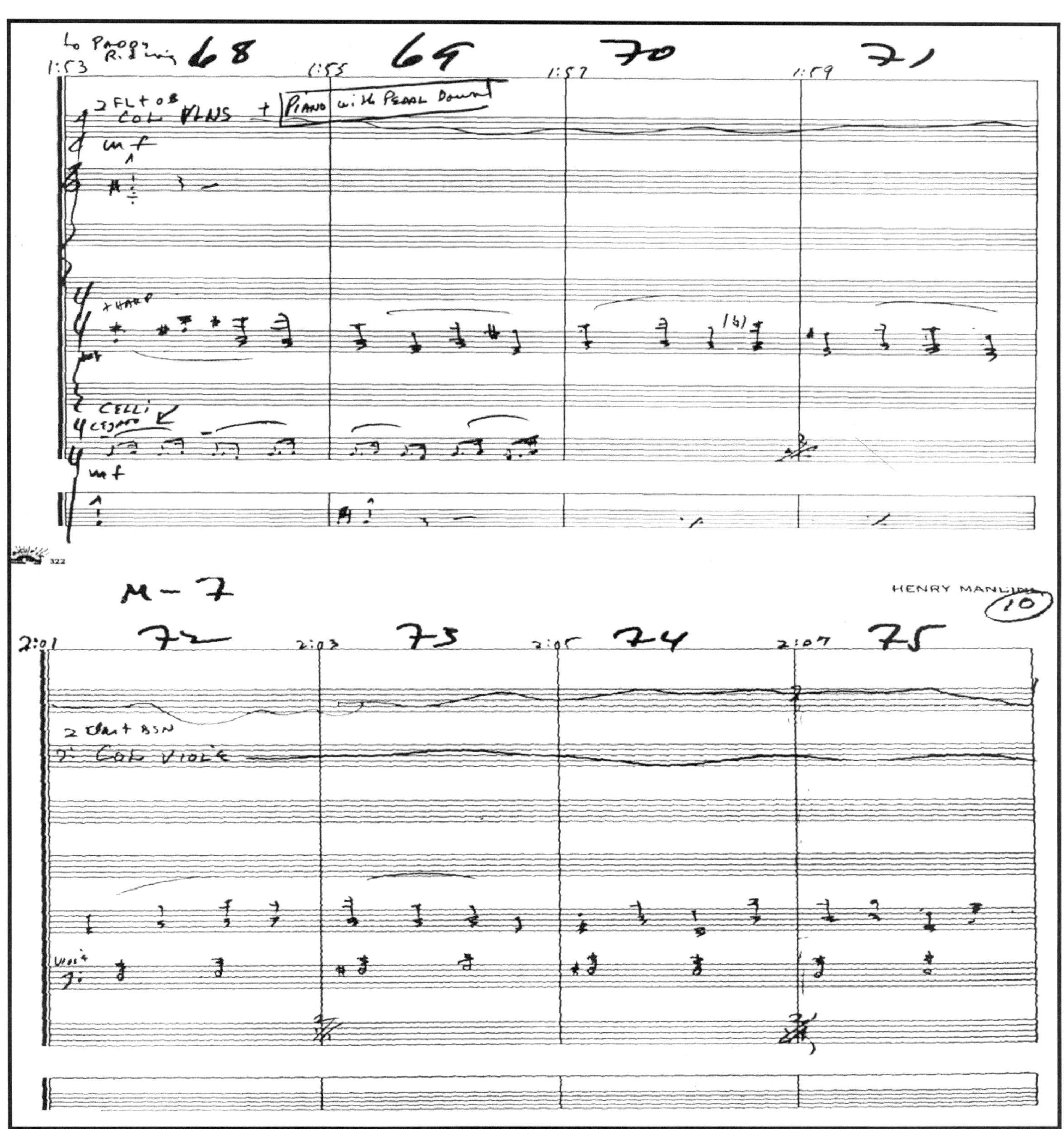
Lo Progres Rigging 68
1:53
69
1:55
70
1:57
71
1:59
2 FLt OB
COL VLNS + PIANO with PEDAL Down
mf
+HARP
mf
CELLI
sustain
mf
M-7
HENRY MANCINI
10
2:01
72
2:03
73
2:05
74
2:07
75
2 Clar + BSN
COL VIOLE
VIOL

Fire on Drogheda!

:26
:28
:30
:32
Eng. Hn.
Cl.
Bsn.
(a4)
3 Hn.
f
Vln.
f
f
Va.
Vc.
f
Cb.
Timp. tacet
Pno. R. H.
+ 8vb L. H.
Timp.
Pno.

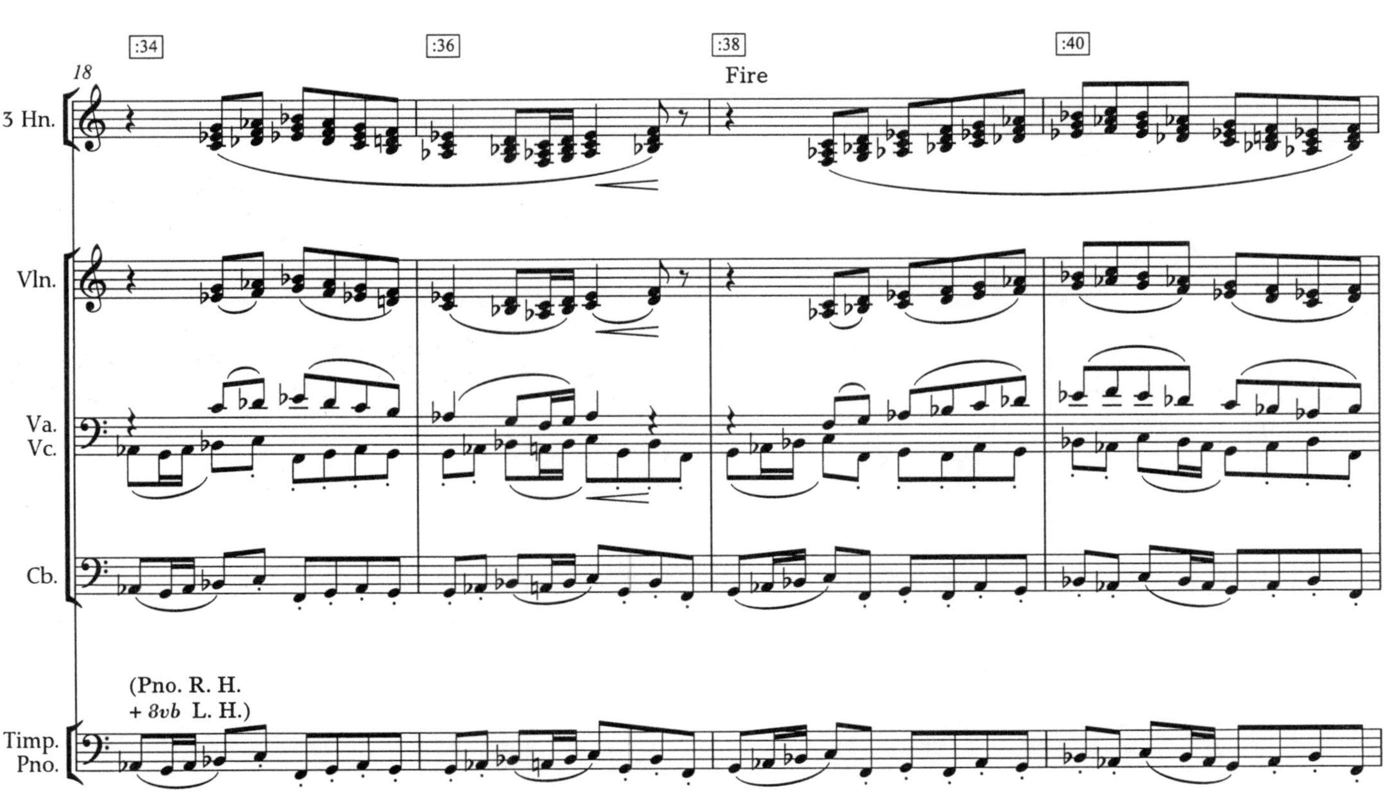
:34
:36
:38
:40
Fire
3 Hn.
Vln.
Va.
Vc.
Cb.
(Pno. R. H.
+ 8vb L. H.)
Timp.
Pno.

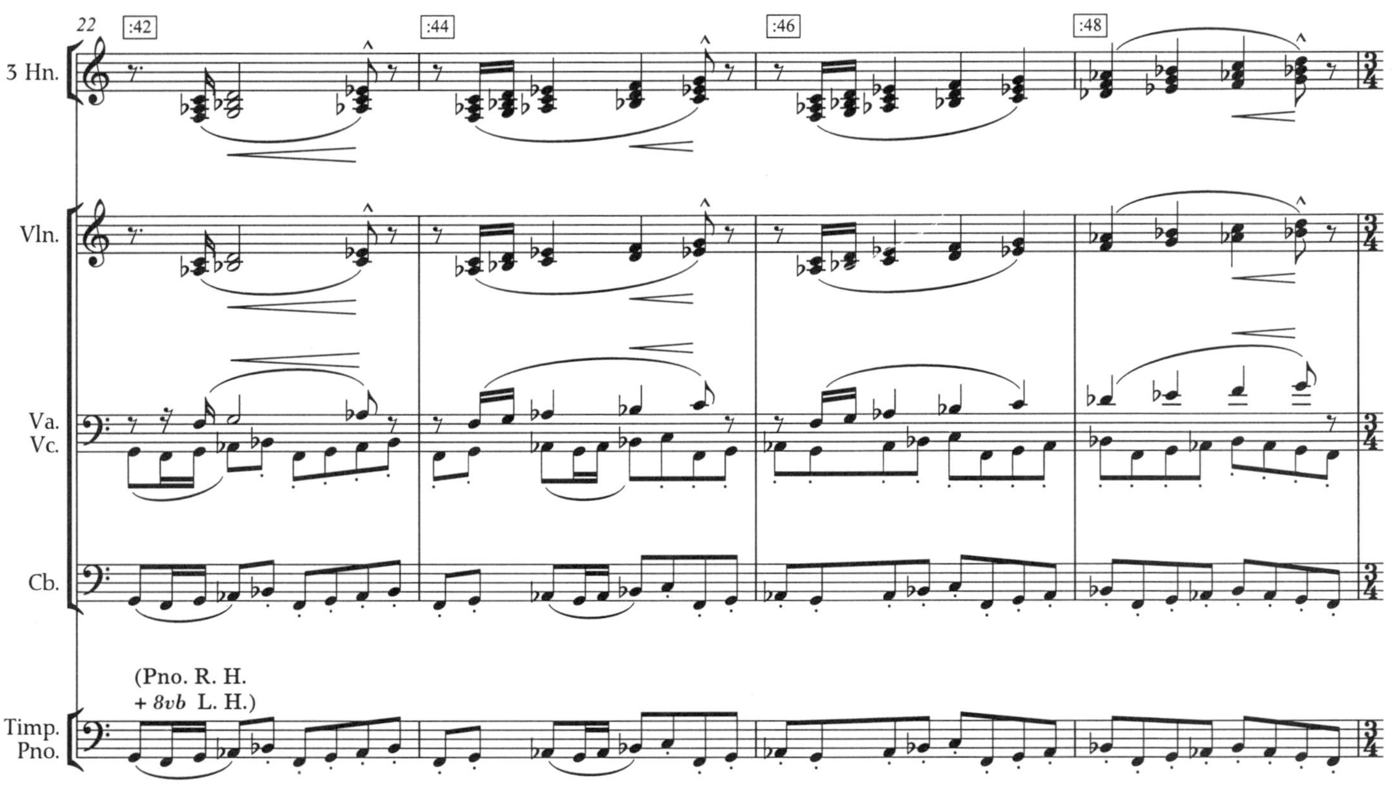
22
:42
:44
:46
:48
3 Hn.
Vln.
Va.
Vc.
Cb.
(Pno. R. H.
+ 8vb L. H.)
Timp.
Pno.

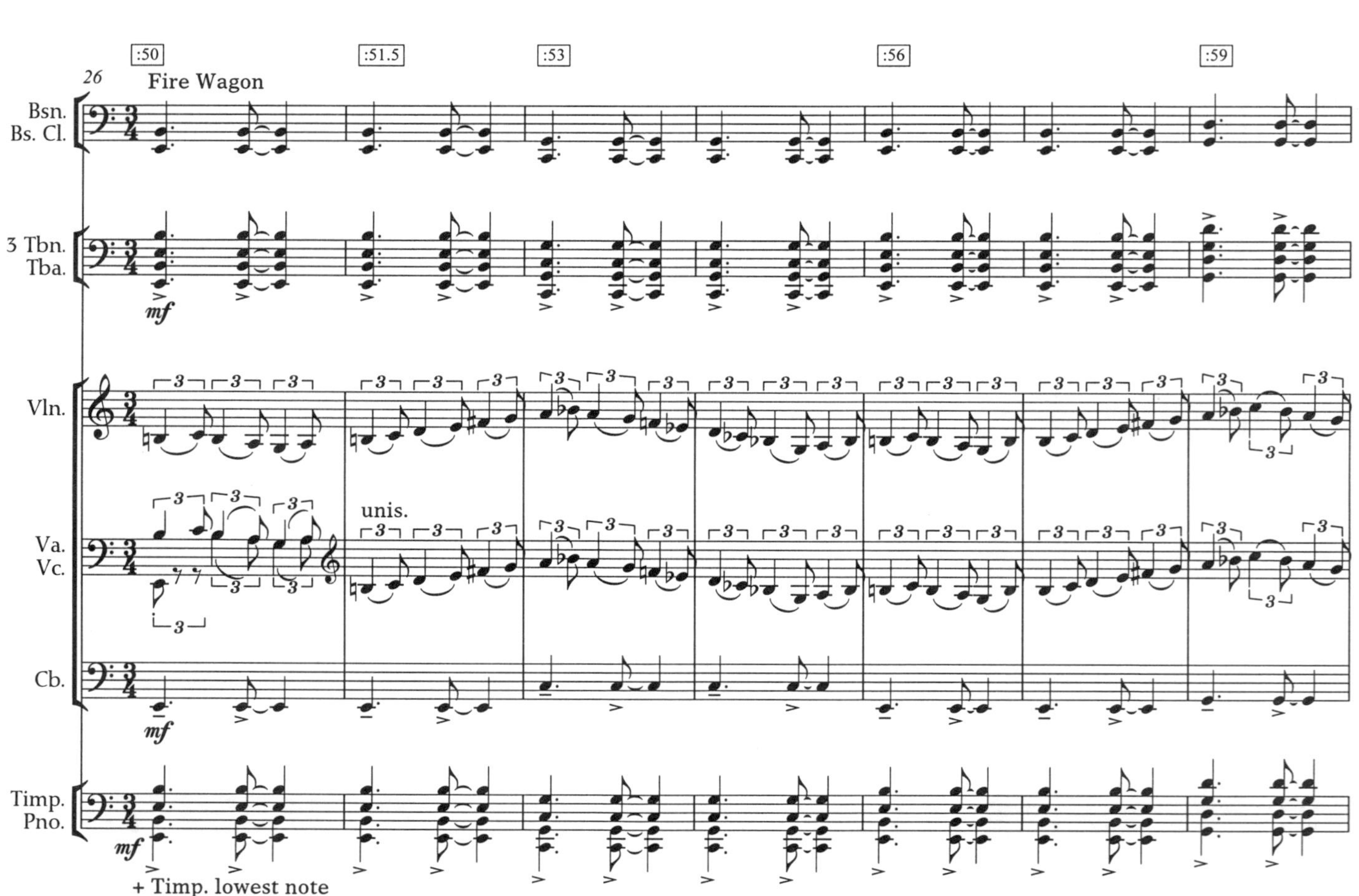
:50
:51.5
:53
:56
:59
26
Fire Wagon
Bsn.
Bs. Cl.
3 Tbn.
Tba.
mf
Vln.
unis.
Va.
Vc.
Cb.
mf
Timp.
Pno.
mf
+ Timp. lowest note

1:02
1:05
33
2 Fl.
Eng. Hn.
Cl.
Fl., a2
Eng. Hn. &
Cl., a2
f
a2
Bsn.
Bs. Cl.
3 Tbn.
Tba.
Vln.
sim.
(unis.)
Va.
Vc.
Cb.
Timp.
Pno.
(Timp. lowest note)
1:08
1:11
38
(a2)
(Timp. lowest note)

1:14
(Fl. a2, Eng. Hn.
Cl., Hn. 3)
(a2)
1:17
2 Fl.
Eng. Hn.
Cl.
Hn. 3
Bsn.
Bs. Cl.
Hn. 1 & 2, a2
2 Hn.
3 Tbn.
Tba.
Hp.
Pno.
Vln.
Va.
Vc.
Cb.
Vib.
Ped.

2 Fl.
Eng. Hn.
Cl.
Hn. 3
Bsn.
Bs. Cl.
2 Hn.
3 Tbn.
Tba.
Hp.
Pno.
Vln.
Va.
Vc.
Cb.
Timp.
Vib.
46
1:20
1:23
(a2)
Bsn.
(Vibes)
Timp.
Vc.
50
1:26
1:29
1:32
Bsn.
(Vc.)
+ Va.
Va.
Vc.
Cb.
Timp.

1:35
1:38
1:41
56
2 Fl.
Ob.
2 Cl.
Bsn.
a5
Vln.
Va.
Vc.
Cb.
div.
Timp.

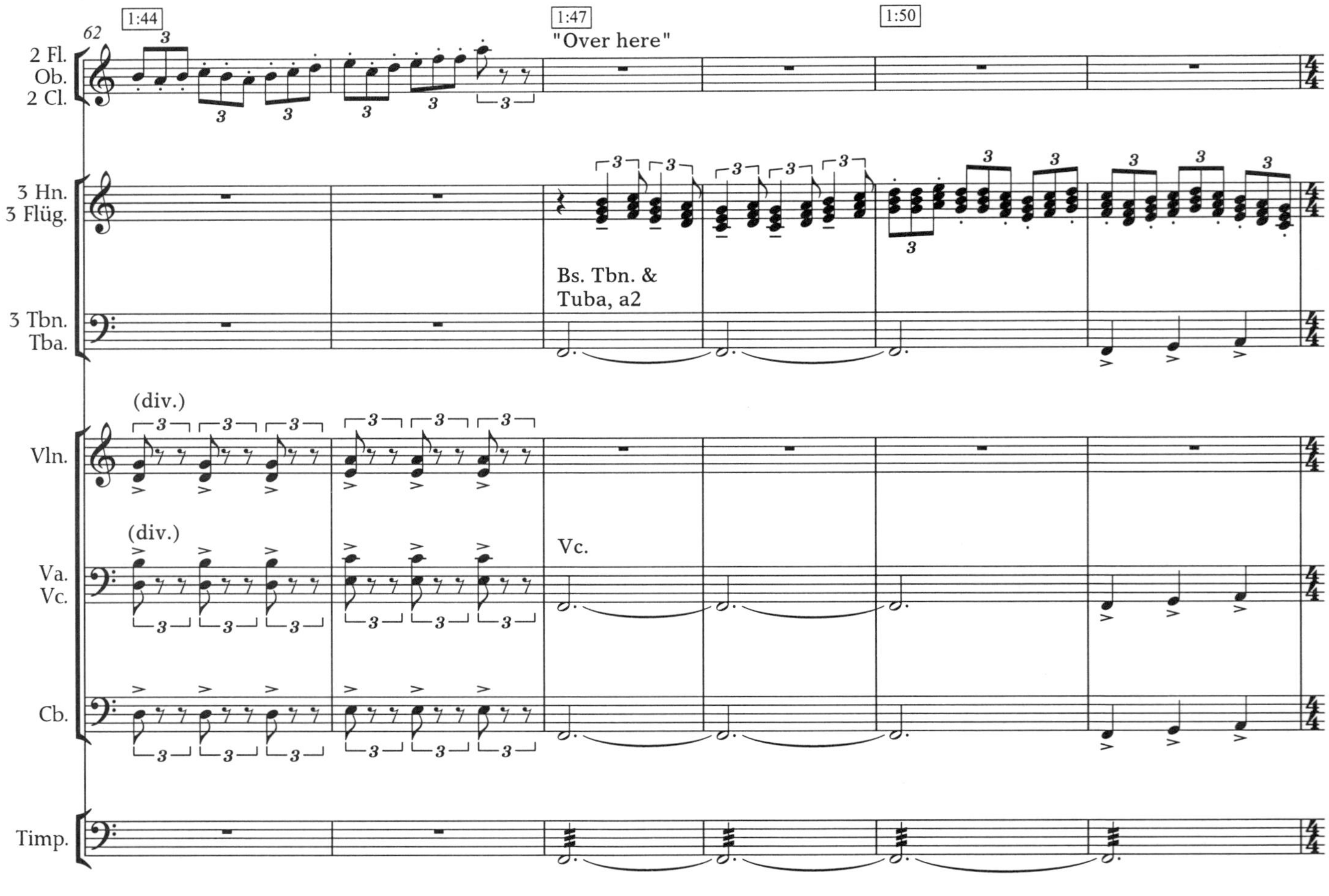

1:44
1:47
1:50
62
2 Fl.
Ob.
2 Cl.
"Over here"
3 Hn.
3 Flüg.
3 Tbn.
Tba.
Bs. Tbn. &
Tuba, a2
Vln.
(div.)
Va.
Vc.
(div.)
Vc.
Cb.
Timp.

To Paddy riding
1:53
1:55
1:57
1:59
2 Fl.
Ob.
Pno.
Hp.
a4
mf
Pno.
Ped.
3 Hn.
3 Flüg.
Vln.
mf
Va.
Vc.
(Vc.)
Cb.
Timp.
68

2:01
2:03
2:05
2:07
2:09
2 Fl.
Ob.
Pno.
Hp.
(a5)
2 Cl.
Bsn.
a3
Vln.
Va.
Vc.
+ Va.
Cb.
Timp.
72

2:11
Paddy's horse rears
2:12.5
2:13.5
Tree starts to fall
2:15.5
2 Fl., a2
+ Cl. 1 8vb
mf
2 Fl., a2
Cl. 1
Ob.
Cl. 2
Cl. 2, Ob. a2
Ob.
+ Cl. 2 8vb
mf
77
2 Fl.
Ob.
2 Cl.
Bsn.
mf
sfz sfz sfz sfz
1. sfz
3 Tpt.
2. & sfz
3., a2
3. sfz
sfz
a3
3 Hn.
Pno. tacet
Tbn: 1.
3 Tbn.
Tba.
Pno.
sfz
2. & 3., a2
unis.
Vln.
Vln.
Va.
Va.
Vc.
Cb.
Timp.
sfz
2:17.5
2:18.5
Tree hits, engulfs Paddy
2:20
2:21.5
81
2 Fl.
Ob.
2 Cl.
Bsn.
sfz
sfz
3 Tpt.
(a3)
3 Hn.
a3
1. & 2., a2
3 Tbn.
Tba.
3.
Tba.
Vln.
Va.
Vc.
Cb.
+ Pno. lowest 8ve
Timp.
Pno.

2:23
Fl. tacet
Ob.
2 Cl.
2:25
2:27
2:29
85
Fire line
2 Fl.
Ob.
2 Cl.
Bsn.
Tpt.
3 Tpt.
3 Hn.
sfz Hns. a3
3 Tbn.
Tba.
unis.
Vln.
Va.
f
sim.
Vc.
f
sim.
Cb.
(+ Pno. lowest 8ve)
+ Hp.
Timp.
Pno.
Hp.
2:31
(Ob.
2 Cl.)
2:33
2:35
2:37
2:37.8
Back to the ranch
89
2 Fl.
Ob.
2 Cl.
Bsn.
3 Tpt.
3 Hn.
(Hn. a3)
3 Tbn.
Tba.
Vln.
Vla.
Vc.
Cb.
Timp.
Pno.
Hp.

Example 10
M–24 Luke and Meggie (Episode II)
⊙ **CD Track 10**

Love has developed between Luke and Meggie. This is the first occurrence of their theme. The opening of this cue is super–sensitive. The muted piano, with sustaining pedal down, gives us a soft, effective entrance. I waited until Luke makes his move to kiss Meggie before I introduce the theme, carried by the alto flute. We go along to the point where we think that he is going to make his big move. Instead, at 1:42.6 he backs off with a soft, "Good night, Meghan." The solo bass clarinet mirrors her confusion at Luke's attitude. We go out as we came in, with the muted piano, as Meggie slowly goes into the house.

Production: **THE THORNBIRDS**   Production #: 167602
Cue: **M - 24 "LUKE AND MEGGIE"**

ABS SMPTE #(df)	REL. TIME:		
			AFTER THE DANCE, LUKE BRINGS MEGGIE HOME, AND THEY STAND TALKING OUTSIDE THE HOUSE. HE TELLS HER ABOUT HER AMBITIONS AND GOALS, AND TELLS HER HE NEEDS SOMEONE TO SHARE IT WITH AND TO LOVE HIM. WITHOUT SAYING ANYTHING, SHE STARTS TOWARD THE STEPS.
	0:00.0		START MUSIC AS SHE STARTS UP THE STEPS
	0:02.6		HE STARTS UP AFTER HER
	0:11.5		THEY REACH THE TOP OF THE STEPS AND MOVE TOWARD THE DOOR
	0:18.3	CUT	CLOSER SHOT AS THEY STOP BESIDE THE DOOR AND TURN TOWARD EACH OTHER
	0:21.4		MEGGIE GLANCES OVER AT THE DOOR AND NOTICES THAT HIS ARM IS BLOCKING HER ACCESS TO IT
	0:24.8		HE VERY SLOWLY STARTS TO LEAN IN TOWARD HER
	0:29.1		HE KISSES HER ON THE CHEEK
	0:33.0		SHE PUTS HER HEAD BESIDE HIS AS HE NUZZLES HER CHEEK AND HER NECK
	0:40.6	CUT	REVERSE ANGLE, FAVORING LUKE, AS HE CONTINUES
	0:45.6		HE PULLS BACK AND LOOKS AT HER
	0:49.4		HE SAYS, SOTTO VOCE: "GOD, YOU ARE BEAUTIFUL."
	0:51.1	CUT	EOL. MEGGIE LOOKING AT HIM STRANGELY
	0:55.4	CUT	LUKE STILL LOOKING AT HER
	0:56.5		LUKE: "HOW MANY TIMES YOU BEEN IN LOVE?"
	0:58.2		PAUSE
	0:58.6	CUT	MEGGIE
	1:04.8		MEGGIE: "ONLY ONCE."
	1:06.4	CUT	LUKE
	1:07.6		LUKE: "WELL, WHOEVER HE WAS, HE WAS A FOOL TO LET YOU GO."

1:10.4   CUT   EOL. MEGGIE. . .

1:11.5   . . .AS SHE SMILES, AND HE DOES ALSO.

1:14.7   CUT   LUKE LOOKING AT HER

1:18.6   CUT   MEGGIE LOOKING AT HIM

1:21.4   HE STARTS TO LEAN SLOWLY INTO TOWARD HER AGAIN

1:24.6   THIS TIME HE GOES FOR THE OTHER CHEEK. . .

1:29.8   . . .AND THEN DOWN TO THE NECK

1:30.6   SHE PUTS HER HANDS ON HIS SHOULDERS AS SHE STARTS TO GET TURNED-ON

1:40.5   HE PULLS BACK FROM HER, AND SHE MOVES TOWARD HIM, TRYING TO TOUCH HER LIPS TO HIS

1:42.6   HE SAYS SOFTLY: **"GOOD NIGHT, MEGGIN."**

1:43.8   EOL

1:46.7   SHE PULLS BACK SLIGHTLY AND THEY LOOK AT EACH OTHER

1:57.3   HE SLOWLY TURNS AND STARTS TO WALK OFF

2:02.6   SHE TURNS HER HEAD AND LOOKS AFTER HIM

2:05.3   CUT   FS OF THE PORCH, AS HE STARTS DOWN THE STEPS VERY SLOWLY, HIS HANDS IN HIS POCKETS, AND SHE STANDS BY THE DOOR LOOKING AFTER HIM.

2:14.2   SHE TURNS BACK TOWARD THE DOOR. . .

2:15.7   . . .AND STARTS TO MOVE TOWARD IT

2:17.9   SHE PUTS HER HANDS ON THE KNOB AND STOPS. . .

2:19.3   . . .THEN TURNS AND LOOKS BACK AT LUKE AGAIN

2:24.5   SHE STARTS TO OPEN THE DOOR BEHIND HER

2:28.3   SHE CLOSES THE DOOR BEHIND HER

2:30.0   END MUSIC IN FADE-OUT TO COMMERCIAL. (1/2 SECOND BEFORE FULL OUT.)

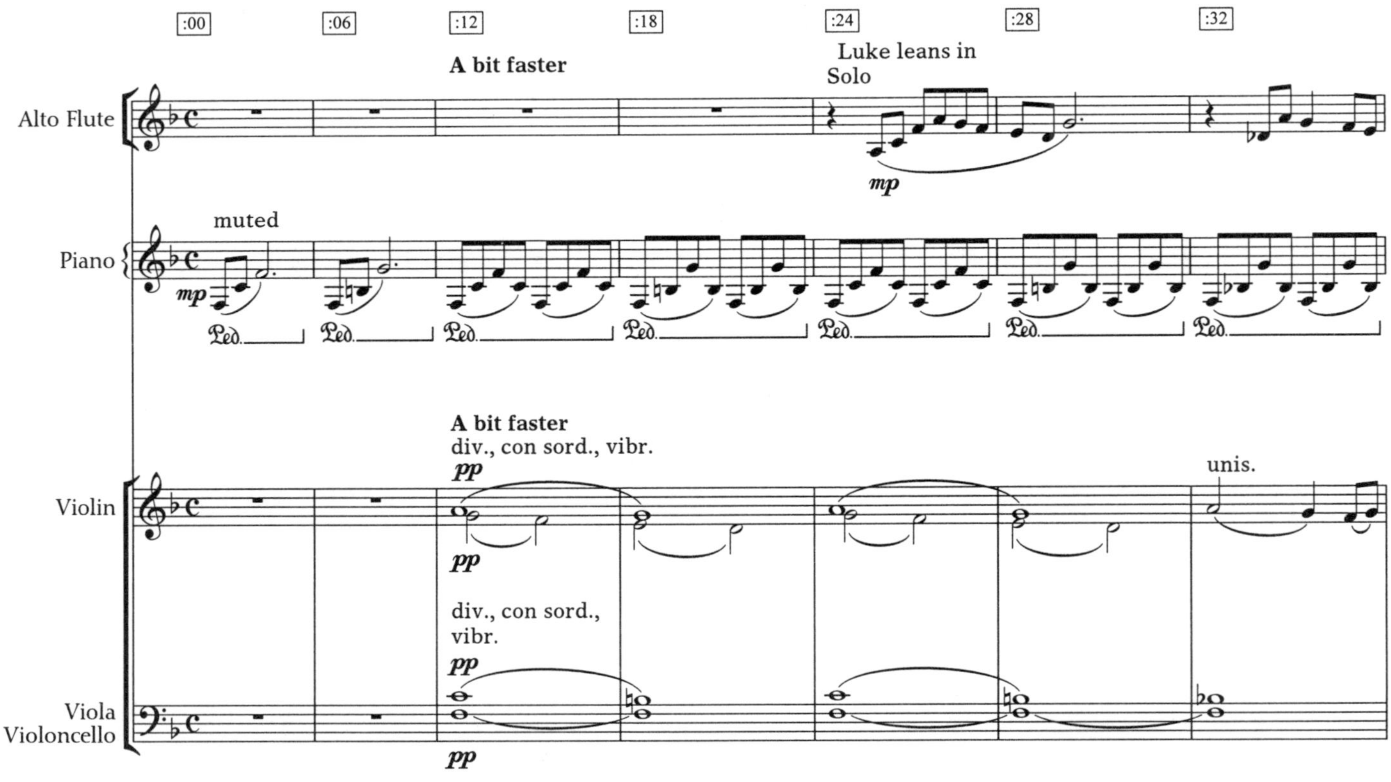
M - 24 Episode II
Luke and Meggie
:00 :06 :12 :18 :24 :28 :32
A bit faster
Luke leans in
Solo
Alto Flute
mp
Piano
muted
mp
Ped. Ped. Ped. Ped. Ped. Ped. Ped.
A bit faster
div., con sord., vibr.
pp
Violin
pp
unis.
div., con sord., vibr.
pp
Viola
Violoncello
pp

8 :36 :40 :44 :48 :52 :56 1:00
A. Fl.
Hp.
mp
Pno.
Ped. Ped. Ped. Ped. Ped.
(div.)
Vln.
unis.
dolce
(div.)
Va. div.
Va.
Vc.
Vc. div.
Cb.

15
1:04   1:08   1:12   1:16   1:20   1:24
A. Fl.
p
Hp.
Vln.
Va., unis.
Va.
Vc.
(div.)
div.
Cb.
1:28   1:32   1:36   1:40   1:42
"Goodnight Meggie"
21
Vln.
(unis.)
Va.
Vc.
Cb.
25
1:44   1:48   1:52   1:56
Bs. Cl.
mp
Vln.
(unis.)
pp
pp
Va.
Vc.
pp
Cb.
pp
29
2:19   2:24   2:30
Bs. Cl.
Pno.
Ped.   Ped.   Ped.   Ped.   Ped.

Example 11
M–29 Arrival at the Vatican (Episode II)
⊙ CD Track 11

The timings and music pretty much speak for themselves in this piece. Ralph is awed by his first view of the place he has dreamed of all of his life. The approach to the music is classical in keeping with the visual grandness of the Vatican.

Production: **THE THORNBIRDS**   Production #: 167602
Cue: **M - 24 "LUKE AND MEGGIE"**

ABS SMPTE #(df)	REL. TIME:		
	0:00.0		START MUSIC (SEGUE FROM M-28) ON CUT TO AN ESTABLISHING SHOT OF ROME. THIS IS A VIEW LOOKING UNDER A BRIDGE, AND WE CAN SEE ST. PETER'S IN THE BACKGROUND.
	0:02.0		CAMERA STARTS TO ZOOM IN SLOWLY ON ST. PETER'S
	0:10.8		A CAPTION FADES IN , READING: "THE VATICAN"
	0:16.8		CENTER OF DISS. TO A MOVING SHOT OF THE COLUMNS IN FRONT OF THE COLISEUM
	0:24.7	CUT	RALPH RIDING IN A CARRIAGE WITH THE ARCHBISHOP AS RALPH RUBBERNECKS WITH HIS MOUTH OPEN
	0:26.4		HE LOOKS OVER AT THE ARCHBISHOP AND SMILES
	0:29.8	CUT	A VERY NARROW STREET, LINED WITH SWISS GUARDS, APPARENTLY NEAR THE BACK OF ST. PETER'S. WE SEE THEIR CAR COMING DOWN THE STREET TOWARD US
	0:36.8	CUE	RALPH AND THE ARCHBISHOP, AS RALPH WATCHES EVERYTHING EAGERLY
	0:39.9		THE ARCHBISHOP POINTS TO SOMETHING AND RALPH LOOKS
	0:41.1	CUT	THEIR POV: A MOVING SHOT LOOKING UP PAST THE TREE TOPS, AS THE BASILICA OF ST. PETER'S LOOMS IMPRESSIVELY
	0:47.7		CENTER OF DISS. TO THE INTERIOR, AS WE SEE RALPH AND THE ARCHBISHOP WALKING TOWARD US DOWN A MARBLE CORRIDOR
	0:59.4		THEY ROUND A CORNER AND COME FACE-TO-FACE WITH A CARDINAL
	1:00.3		THE ARCHBISHOP KNEELS TO KISS HIS RING
	1:05.5		RALPH DOES LIKEWISE
	1:09.9		THEY ALL CONTINUE ON. . .
	1:11.7		. . .AND RALPH TURNS TO LOOK BACK AT THE CARDINAL
	1:14.3		THE ARCHBISHOP GETS RALPH'S ATTENTION BY PUTTING HIS HAND ON RALPH'S SHOULDER
	1:16.3		THEY CONTINUE ON DOWN THE CORRIDOR
	1:19.8		CENTER OF DISS. TO A MOVING SHOT OF SOME VERY ORNAMENTAL WALLS, COVERED WITH PAINTINGS AND TAPESTRIES
	1:26.0		CENTER OF DISS. TO A LARGLE MARBLE ROOM GUARDED BY SWISS GUARDS.

1:28.4		WE SEE RALPH WALKING INTO IT FROM THE BACKGROUND. HE WALKS SLOWLY, LOOKING ALL AROUND AT ITS SPLENDOR
1:42.9		HE STOPS IN FRONT OF CAMERA, PUTTING HIS HAND ON ONE OF THE MARBLE COLUMNS AND LOOKS UP AT SOMETHING
1:44.1	CUT	HIS POV: THE MAGNIFICENT CEILING OF THE BASILICA
1:49.5	CUT	RALPH LOOKING UP AT IT, AS HE CONTINUES ON
1:53.0		THE ARCHBISHOP STEPS INTO THE SCENE, LOOKING AFTER HIM
1:57.8		A MONA-LISA SMILE CROSSES HIS FACE
1:58.8	CUT	END MUSIC BACK TO DROGHEDA. WE SEE FIONA SITTING AT A TABLE, USING AN ADDING-MACHINE (NO DIALOGUE TO CONTEND WITH.)

Arrival at the Vatican

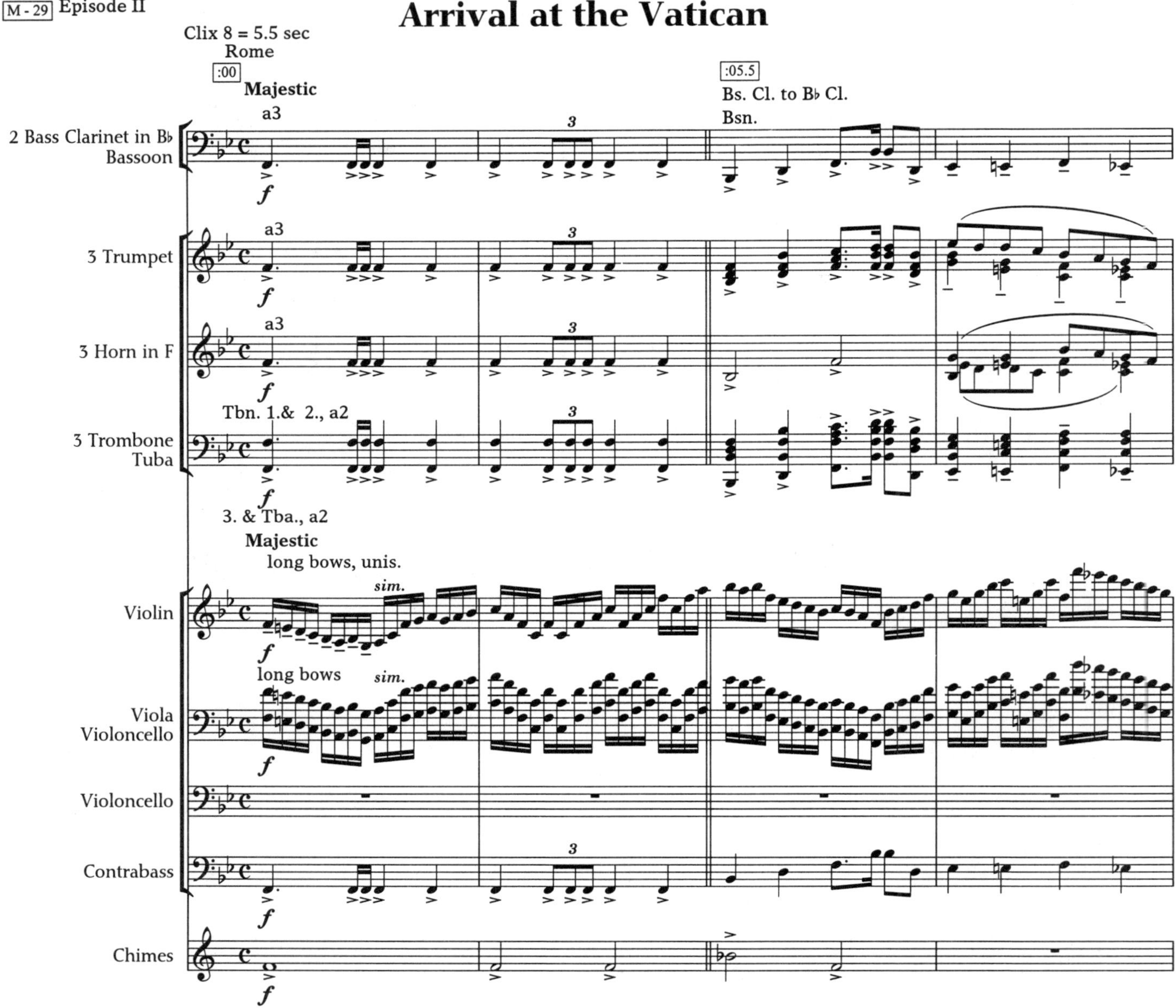

Cl. 2
Bsn.
Tpt.
Hn.
Tbn.
Tba.
Vln.
Va.
Vc.
Vc.
Cb.
a3
a3
:11
:16.5
:22
:27.5
div.
pizz.
mp

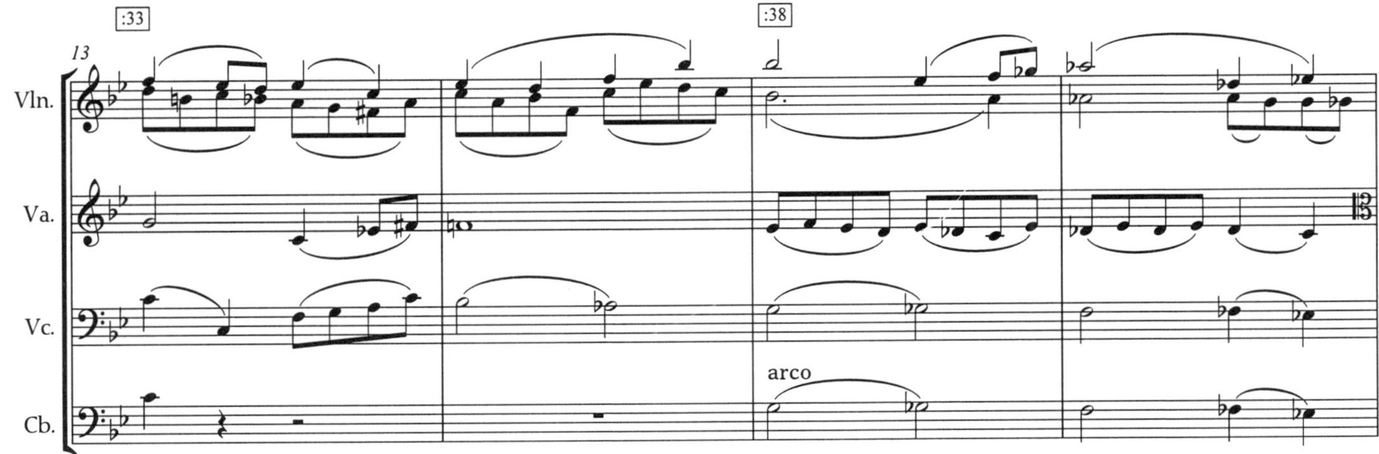

1:11.5
1:17
1:22.5
26
2 Fl.
Eng. Hn.
Cl. 1
Fl. a2
Eng. Hn.
& Cl. a2
Cl. 2
Bsn.
a2
a2
Picc. Tpt.
Vln.
Va.
Vc.
Cb.
32
1:28
2 Fl.
Eng. Hn.
Cl. 1
(a2)
Cl. 2
Bsn.
Soli
1:33.5
Vln.
Soli
Va.
Vc.
div.
unis.
Cb.
1:39
1:44.5
1:50
1:58.5
Clix off
Rit.
Back to
Drogheda
37
Vln.
Va. unis.
Va.
Vc.
Vc. div.
Cb.

Example 12
M–18 The Letter (Episode III)
⊙ CD Track 12

As you can see by scanning the timings, not too much happens during the first part of the scene. Music for this kind of scene falls into the undefinable category of "neutral." In this case it's "bringing in the morning mail" – neutral. At :36.3 Ralph sees that one of the letters is from Meggie. A bit of their theme enters, reminding us that the flame has not yet gone out.

Here again, the sparse approach works well for the scene.

Production: **THE THORNBIRDS** Production #: 167601
Cue: **M - 18 "THE LETTER"**

REL. TIME:

Time	Cut	Action
0:00.0		START MUSIC ON FADE-IN FROM COMMERCIAL. THIS IS A FADE-IN TO AN ESTABLISHING SHOT OF THE LARGE CHURCH.
0:05.1	CUT	THE INTERIOR, AS WE SEE RALPH IN HIS STUDY STANDING BY THE WINDOW DEEP IN THOUGHT
0:09.1		AN AIDE STARTS INTO THE ROOM CARRYING THE MAIL
0:11.7		RALPH LOOKS OVER AT HIM AS HE STARTS TOWARD THE DESK
0:14.9		THE PRIEST PUTS THE MAIL ON THE DESK IN FRONT OF CAMERA. . .
0:16.5		. . .AND STARTS TO WALK OUT AGAIN
0:17.3		RALPH: **"THANK YOU, FATHER."**
0:18.3		EOL, AS THE PRIEST CONTINUES ON OUT. . .
0:19.6		. . .AND RALPH STARTS WALKING SLOWLY TOWARD THE DESK
0:29.2		HE STOPS AT THE DESK, PULLS THE MAIL OVER TO HIM AND BEGINS GOING THRU IT LETTER BY LETTER
0:36.3		HE PAUSES AS HE SEES THAT THE LETTER HE HAS JUST PICKED UP IS FROM MEGGIE
0:41.8		HE STARTS TO TURN AND MOVE AWAY SLOWLY AS HE CONTINUES TO LOOK AT THE LETTER
0:51.8		HE STARTS TO OPEN IT
0:54.9		HE PULLS OUT THE LETTER AND STARTS TO UNFOLD IT
0:56.9		HE STARTS TO READ IT
1:02.1	CUT	END MUSIC TO LUDDIE STANDING BESIDE THE ROAD, AS LUKE COMES DRIVING IN FAST
1:09.6		HE STOPS IN FRONT OF THE HOUSE
1:14.4		HE JUMPS OUT AND STORMS TOWARD THE HOUSE

The Letter

Fade in church:
Clarinet in B♭
Solo
mp
3 Horn in F
a3
mf
Harp
mp
Violin
div. a3, con sord.
mp
Viola
div.
mf
mf
Violoncello
div.
mf
mf
:00
:05
:10
:15
:20
:23.5
:25
:27.5
:30
:33
Rit.
A. Fl.
Ob.
Cl.
Ob.
(Cl.)
Hn.
(a3)
Vln. I
(div. a3)
Rit.
9
:36.3
:39
:42
:45
:48
:51
:54
:57
1:02.1
15
A. Fl.
Ob.
Cl.
A. Fl.
(Ob.)
Bsn.
p
Back to
Queensland
Pno.
muted
Ped.
Ped.
Ped.
Ped.
Va.
Vc.
div. a3
3 desks, con sord.

Meggie's new baby is brought into the world accompanied by a light and airy theme. The celesta, song bells and harp form the ornamentation behind the violins' melody. The strings carry on alone at :24 and continue until :33 giving way to the woodwinds alone. This was done because at :38.1 I wanted to have a fresh entrance from the strings to cover Ralph's sitting quietly in the garden, lost in prayer. The mood is quite different from the opening music. We are back to Meggie and her baby at :58.8. The return to a major key plus the song bellls bring us back to a lighter conclusion.

Production: **THE THORNBIRDS**　　Production #: 167603
Cue: **M - 20 "NEW KID IN TOWN"**

ABS SMPTE #(df)　　　　REL. TIME:

0:00.0		START MUSIC ON PLAY-IN FROM COMMERCIAL. THIS IS AN ESTABLISHING SHOT OF THE HIMMELHOCH HOUSE AS WE HEAR THE BABY CRYING.
0:05.6	CUT	MEGGIE IN BED AS WE SEE THE DOCTOR ROLLING DOWN HIS SLEEVES.
0:09.4		THE MIDWIFE STARTS TO CROSS IN FRONT OF CAMERA AND OUT OF THE ROOM CARRYING THE NEWBORN INFANT.
0:12.5		SHE STOPS JUST OUTSIDE AND HOLDS THE BABY UP FOR ANNE AND LUDDIE AS THEY OOOH AND AHHH OVER IT
0:14.5		LUDDIE CHUCKLES AND SAYS: **"WELL, THERE'S NOTHING WRONG WITH YOU, IS THERE? HEY, SHOOO."**
0:19.0		THE MIDWIFE PUTS THE BABY INTO RALPH'S ARMS AS LUDDIE SAYS: **"HUSH UP, HUSH UP."**
0:21.2		THE BABY BEGINS TO SCREAM LOUDLY
0:24.2		ANNE SAYS: **"I THINK WE COULD ALL USE A LITTLE REST, LUDDIE."**
0:26.9		EOL, AS THE BABY CONTINUES TO CRY. . .
0:27.9		. . .AND RALPH STARTS TO WALK SLOWLY DOWN THE HALL WITH THE BABY
0:38.1		CENTER OF DISS. TO A MLS OF RALPH SITTING AT A TABLE IN THE GARDEN. HE SITS QUIETLY WITHOUT MOVING, EITHER IN PRAYER OR DEEP IN THOUGHT.
0:48.7	CUT	MCU OF RALPH, HIS LIPS MOVING SILENTLY IN PRAYER
0:58.8	CUT	MEGGIE IN BED, HOLDING HER BABY, AS IT CONTINUES TO CRY
1:02.0		RALPH APPEARS IN THE DOORWAY AND STARTS INTO THE ROOM
1:08.1		HE STOPS BESIDE THE BED AND TICKLES THE BABY UNDER THE CHIN
1:11.4		HE STARTS TO REACH DOWN TO TAKE THE BABY
1:14.3		END MUSIC AS HE PICKS UP THE BABY AND SAYS SOMETHING ABOUT THE BABY LIKELY TO TURN OUT TO BE A SCREAMER

M - 20 Episode III
New Kid in Town
Celesta
Harp
Song Bells
Violin
Viola
Violoncello
p
Ped.
p
unis.
p
div.
p
div.
p
:00
:03
:06
:09
2 Fl.
Ob.
2 Cl.
Cel.
S. Bells
Fl., Cel. S. Bells, a4
Ob. & Cl., a3
Hp.
Vln.
Va.
Vc.
Cb.
div.
pizz.
unis.
:12
:15
:18
:21
5
Ob.
2 Fl.
Cl. 1
Cl. 2
Bsn.
Vln.
Va.
Vc.
Cb.
Fl. a2
Cl. 1
div.
div.
arco
:24
:27
:30
:33
:36
9

Example 14
M–20 Bye Bye Dane (Episode IV)
⊙ CD Track 14

Much has happened since M–20 of Episode III. It is many years later. Meggie has two grown children. The first, Justine (Mare Winningham), is Luke's daughter, a thorn in her mother's side. Her son, Dane (Philip Anglim), is a product of Meggie and Ralph's idyllic tryst at beautiful Matlock Island. Ralph does not know that Dane is his son. To cap things off, Dane has become a priest under his father's guidance.

We are in Greece. Justine is visiting Dane. She had broken up earlier with her boyfriend, Rain (Ken Howard). To make amends she invites him to Greece. They meet, and while they are comsumating their make–up, Dane decides to take a swim.

The opening music has a happy Grecian feeling. As Dane swims, two young local girls decide to join him. (He had left his collar back in the room.)

Everything is gay and light. Dane, however, warns them that the undertow is strong. They are caught up in it and go under. Dane goes to their rescue. They all fail to resurface. The scene is ended by an abrupt silence at 1:04.4.

One problem, however. The day they shot the scene, the ocean did not look especially menacing. The shooting schedule did not permit the crew to sit and wait for Mother Nature to do Her thing.

When we spotted this scene, Stan said that the music was going to have to create most of the undertow. At 1:15.3 I stepped in for Mother Nature.

Production: **THE THORNBIRDS** Production #: 167601
Cue: **M - 20 "BYE BYE DANE"**

ABS SMPTE #(df)	REL. TIME:		
			RAIN HAS COME TO THE BEACH TO BE WITH JUSTINE AND IS WINNING HER OVER, AS HE KISSES HER IN HER BEDROOM
	0:00.0		START MUSIC AFTER THE ABOVE ON CUT TO DANE RUNNING INTO THE OCEAN
	0:03.9		HE PLUNGES HEADLONG INTO IT
	0:09.0	CUT	THE TWO GIRLS LYING ON THE BEACH
	0:11.3		ONE NOTICES THAT DANE HAS GONE INTO THE WATER. . .
	0:13.6		. . .AND GETS THE ATTENTION OF THE OTHER ONE
	0:15.9		THEY WHISPER TO EACH OTHER, MAPPING OUT THEIR STRATEGY
	0:17.8	CUT	THEIR POV: DANE SWIMMING INTO THE OCEAN
	0:24.5	CUT	CLEARER SHOT OF THE GIRLS. . .
	0:28.0		. . .AS THEY GRAB THEIR INFLATED RAFT AND START TO GET TO THEIR FEET
	0:29.6		THEY RUN TOWARD THE WATER
	0:39.1		THEY GET INTO THE WATER AND BEGIN TO PADDLE OUT ON THE RUBBER RAFT
	0:39.7	CUT	DANE SWIMMING, OBLIVIOUS TO THEM
	0:48.2	CUT	THE GIRLS, MOVING TOWARD HIM ON THEIR RAFT
	0:54.4	CUT	DANE, AS HE SEES THEM
	0:56.1	CUT	HIS POV: THE GIRLS APPROACHING AS THEY WAVE AND YELL AT HIM
	0:58.7	CUT	DANE
	0:59.9		HE WAVES AND SAYS: **"HI."**
	1:01.1	CUT	THE GIRLS PADDLING TOWARD HIM
	1:04.6	CUT	DANE
	1:06.9		HE CALLS OUT: **"CAREFUL! THE UNDERTOW'S STRONG!"**
	1:10.6		EOL
	1:11.4	CUT	HIS POV: THE GIRLS PADDLING
	1:15.3		SUDDENLY, THEIR RAFT OVERTURNS, AND THEY BEGIN SCREAMING AND
	1:31.5		HE REACHES THE RAFT. . .
	1:32.4		. . .AND HE LOOKS UNDER IT

Time		Description
1:34.0		HE DIVES UNDER THE WATER TO SEARCH FOR THEM
1:35.9		HE DISAPPEARS OUT OF SIGHT
1:40.4	CUT	MLS OF THE EMPTY RAFT: NO SIGN OF GIRLS OR DANE
1:45.9	CUT	END MUSIC TO JUSTINE AND RAIN IN BED
1:47.2		FIRST DIAL., AS JUSTINE SAYS: **"I DIDN'T DESERVE TO BE THIS HAPPY. . ."**

M - 20   Episode IV

Bye Bye Dane

7
:16.5
:22
2 Fl.
Ob.
Cl. 1
S. Bells
Cl. 2
Bsn.
a2
Hp.
Synth.
Vln.
div.
Va.
Vc.
div. a3
unis.
Cb.

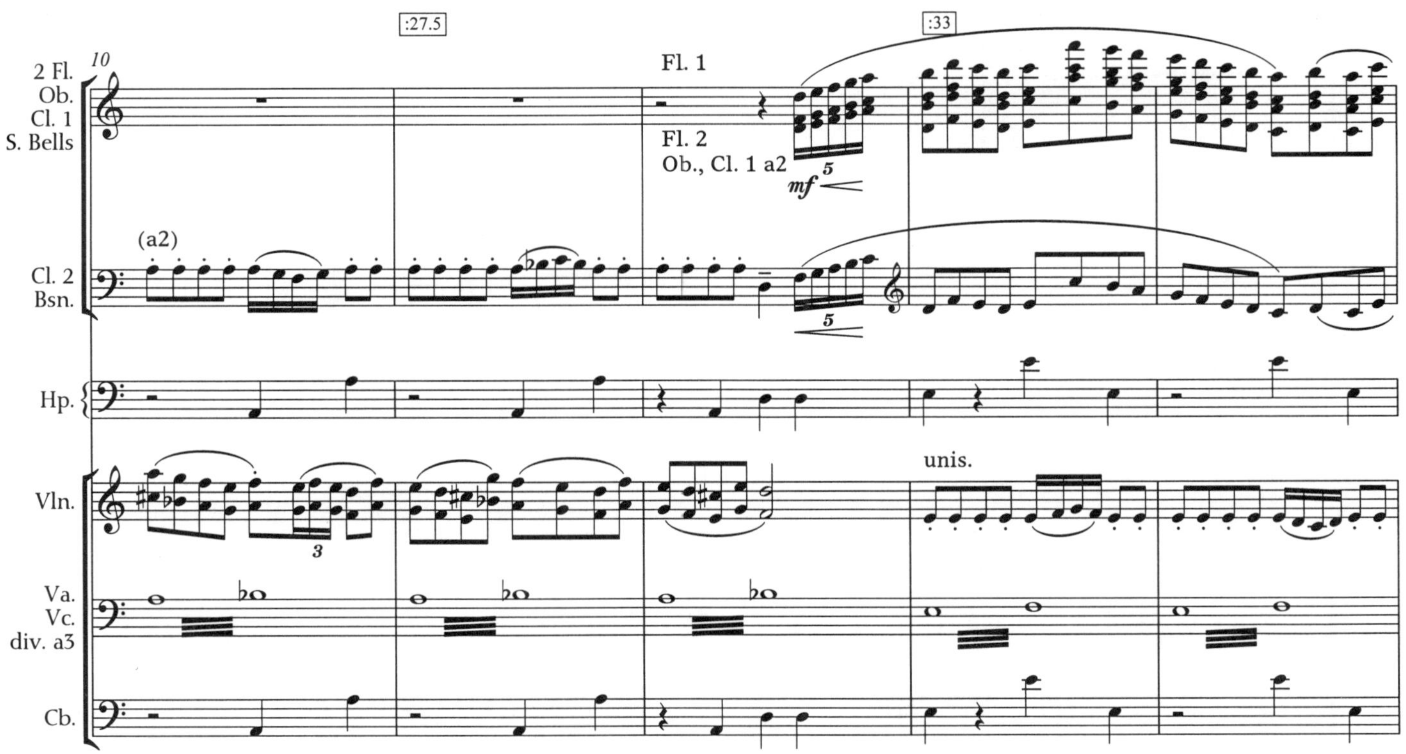
10
:27.5
:33
2 Fl.
Ob.
Cl. 1
S. Bells
Fl. 1
Fl. 2
Ob., Cl. 1 a2
mf
5
Cl. 2
Bsn.
(a2)
5
Hp.
Vln.
3
unis.
Va.
Vc.
div. a3
Cb.

:38.5
:44
:49.5
15
2 Fl.
Ob.
Cl. 1
S. Bells
Cl. 2
Bsn.
(a2)
Hp.
Solo
R. H.
Synth.
L. H.
Vln.
div. a3
Va.
Vc.
div. a3
Cb.
:55
1:00.5
Fl. 1, Ob. a2
Fl. 2, Cl. 1 a2
Cl. 2, Bsn. a2
Fl.,
Ob. a3
20
2 Fl.
Ob.
Cl. 1
S. Bells
Synth.
unis.
Vln.
unis.
Va.
Vc.
div. a3
Cb.
1:06
1:11.5
"careful"
Fl., & Ob., a3
25
2 Fl.
Ob.
Cl. 1
S. Bells
Hp.
Vln.
Va.
Vc.
div. a3
Cb.

109
1:15.3
1:17
1:19
1:21
1:23
1:25
Raft overturns
a3
2 Bs. Cl.
Bsn.
f
a3
3 Hn.
mf
mf 1. & 2., a2
3 Tbn.
Tba.
mf
3. & Tba.
unis.
7
Vln.
Va.
Vc.
Cb.
mf
mf
Pno.
Ped.
Ped.
1:27
1:29
1:31
1:33
(a3)
2 Bs. Cl.
Bsn.
(a3)
3 Hn.
(1. & 2., a2)
3 Tbn.
Tba.
(3.
Tba.)
6
7
Vln.
Va.
Vc.
Cb.
(Pno.)
+ Timp.
Timp.
Pno.
29
35

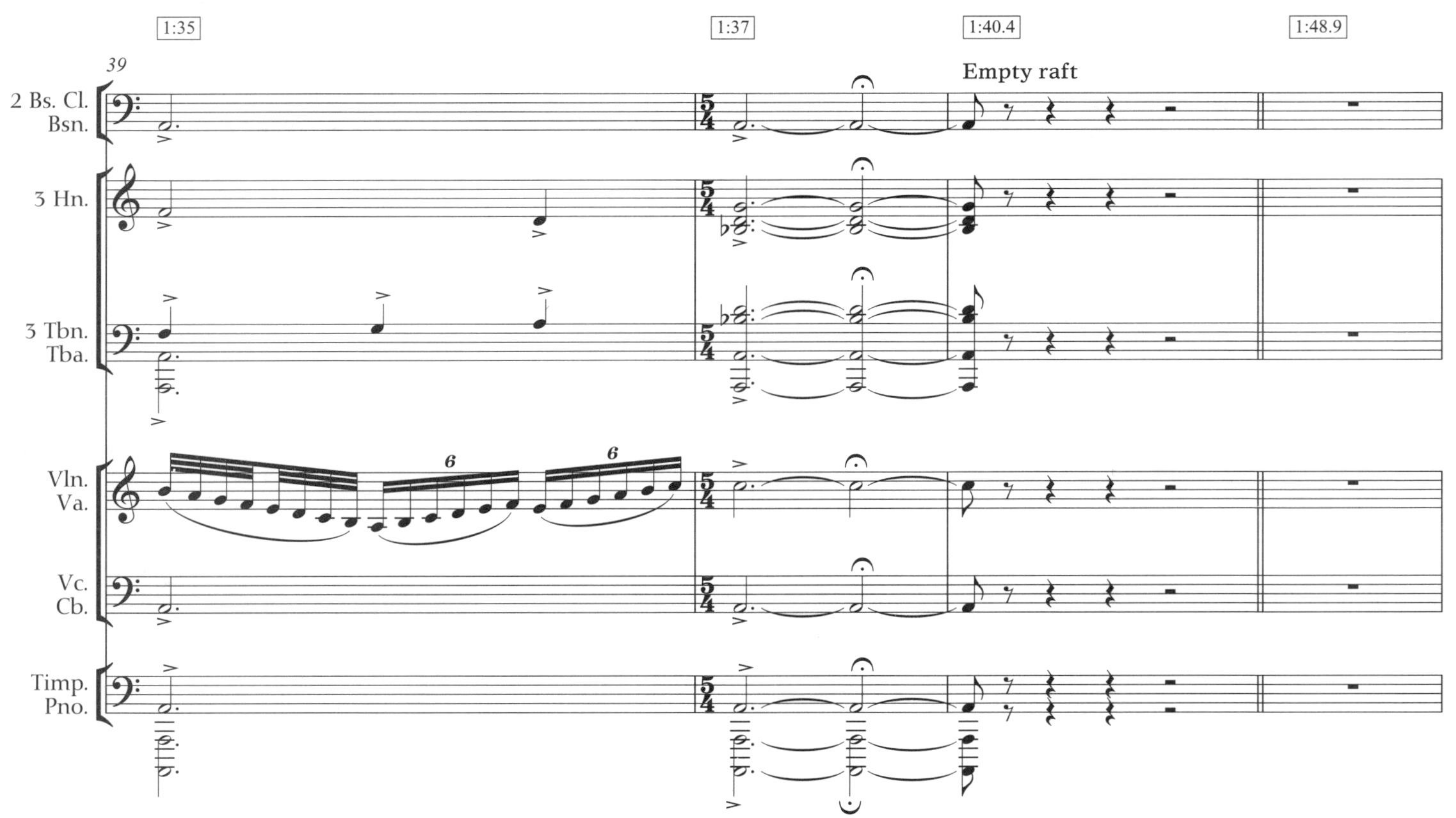

Example 15
M–27 Be Happy (Episode IV)
⊙ CD Track 15

Dane's body has been brought back to Drogheda for burial, after which Meggie tells Ralph, who is looking old and sickly, that he is Dane's father. He is shattered.

The scene, an especially long one, is the beginning of the wrap–up of the film. Fiona, her two sons and Meggie reflect up on the future of Drogheda. Justine and Rain leave, having decided that they were meant to be together. As the jeep drives away, Fi and Meggie exchange looks that reveal that their life–long conflict has been laid to rest. Meggie then seeks out Ralph in the garden. He is very frail now.

"The Thorn Bird Theme," carried by a three–octave woodwind unison opens the scene. The strings form the background. After all of the drama that we have been through the theme evokes a feeling of nostalgia here. The strings take over at 1:06. The material is new, but it seems to be an extension of the theme. I have always been partial to the purity and simplicity of four–part string writing. In this case it works well.

At 1:24.4 Justine appears, ready to leave. The mood changes to a somewhat lighter one. The tempo moves a shade faster, and the orchestration thins out. Solo flute then solo oboe carry us through the goodbyes. Our mood darkens a bit as Meggie asks Rain about Ralph. The woodwinds and basses are just enough to suggest that all is not well with him. The strings re-enter at 2:33.1 as Meggie walks over to Justine for the final emotional parting. Again we have the four-part writing. This time the harmonies are chromatic in keeping with the tone of the action. The music rises over four bars, coming down to just a string quartet as they separate. A solo flute plays over this leading to a woodwind quartet at 3:18. Full strings enter as they get into the jeep and drive off. The bassoon enters at 3:53 as Meggie and Fiona are left alone. The bassoon in this range is a lovely sound.

We switch to a higher register in the strings behind the oboe solo, thus relieving the emotion of the scene. Meggie walks to the garden to find Ralph. We cut to him at 4:25.6. A two-bar introduction leads into "Meggie's Theme," sparsely orchestrated with solo alto flute, muted piano and divided medium low violas and celli. The full strings then add a bit of weight to conclude the scene.

This scene in particular illustrates the very close bond between composition and orchestration. In writing a scene, I am always aware of who is going to play what and where. The interplay of sections and soloists, the register that they will play in, are all part of the same cloth.

Production: **THE THORNBIRDS**   Production #: 167604
Cue: **M - 27 "BE HAPPY"**

ABS SMPTE #(df)	REL. TIME:		
			PLAYON
d3:31:13:02	0:00.00		MUSIC BEGINS ON FADE IN - CAMERA PANNING OVER FS - DROGHEDA
d3:31:26:19	0:13.58		CAMERA PANS OVER HERD OF SHEEP
d3:31:34:25	0:21.79		CAMERFA HOLDS IN FS - SHEEP
d3:31:38:00	0:24.96	CUT	FS - WHAT'S LEFT OF THE CLEARY FAMILY
d3:31:40:03	0:27.06		FIONA: **"WHEN WE GO THERE'LL BE NO ONE. DROGHEDA WILL GO ON WITH NEW PEOPLE. BUT, THERE'LL BE NO ONE LEFT TO REMEMBER WHAT IT WAS LIKE FOR US."**
d3:31:51:28	0:38.91		PAUSE
d3:31:55:25	0:42.81		MEGGIE LOOKS AT HER MOM
d3:32:00:21	0:47.81		MEGGIE LOOKS OFF STAGE TOWARD THE SHEEP
d3:32:02:17	0:49.48		BROTHER: **"WELL, LET'S GO OUT AND SEE HOW DRY THAT GRASS HAS GOT."**
d3:32:08:23	0:53.69		PAUSE
d3:32:08:28	0:55.85		BROTHER LOOKS AT MOM
d3:32:10:26	0:57.79		THE BROTHERS WALK AWAY FROM MEGGIE AND MOM
d3:32:14:02	1:00.99		BROTHER GIVES MEGGIE A KISS ON THE CHEEK
d3:32:16:06	1:03.13		THE MEN CONTINUE TO WALK AWAY
d3:32:17:01	1:03.96		MEGGIE PUTS HER ARM AROUND MOM
d3:32:21:12	1:08.34	CUT	FS - THE MEN DESCENDING THE STEPS
d3:32:27:24	1:14.74		THEY STEP OFF THE BOTTOM STEP AND BROTHER WITH PLAID SHIRT LEANS DOWN TOWARD SUITCASES ON THE GROUND
d3:32:29:03	1:16.04		HE PICKS THEM UP - BROTHER IN BLUE SHIRT STANDS
d3:32:30:27	1:17.84		BROTHER WITH PLAID SHIRT: **"I'LL COME OUT WHEN I GET BACK."**
d3:32:31:29	1:18.91		PAUSE AS THE TWO WALK AWAY FROM THE HOUSE
d3:32:36:22	1:23.68		CAMERA PANS RIGHT FOLLOWING PLAID SHIRT WALKING IN BACK OF JEEP
d3:32:38:01	1:24.99		CAMERA REVEALS BROTHER IN BLUE SHIRT WALKING AWAY FROM CAMERA
d3:32:41:05	1:28.12		PLAID SHIRT PUTS ONE SUITCASE IN THE BACK SEAT

d3:32:42:05	1:29.12	CUT	FS - JUSTINE WALKING INTO VIEW ON THE PORCH TOWARD THE CAMERA
d3:32:47:27	1:34.86		CAMERA PANS RIGHT
d3:32:48:21	1:35.66		CAMERA REVEALS MEGGIE AND MOM AS JUSTINE: **"BYE NANNA FI."**
d3:32:49:26	1:36.83		CAMERA HOLS IN FS - THE THREE LADIES IN PAUSE AS MOM HOLDS HER ARMS OUT
d3:32:50:18	1:37.56		MOM HUGGING JUSTINE: **"COME BACK NEXT CHRISTMAS IF YOU CAN."**
d3:32:52:06	1:39.17		PAUSE
d3:32:52:25	1:39.80		AS THEY RELEASE EMBRACE JUSTINE: **"ALWAYS."**
d3:32:53:15	1:40.47		PAUSE AND FIONA AND JUSTINE HOLD HANDS
d3:32:56:11	1:43.54		JUSTINE LOOKS AT MEGGIE
d3:32:58:18	1:45.57		JUSTINE PUTS HER ARM AROUND MEGGIE
d3:32:59:10	1:46.31		MEGGIE LOOKS AT HER MOM AS THE TWO WALK AWAY FROM FIONA
d3:33:06:25	1:53.75	CUT	FS - ANOTHER PART OF THE HOUSE AS RAIN WALKS INTO VIEW DESCENDING A FEW STEPS AS CAMERA PANS LEFT
d3:33:08:21	1:55.82		CAMERA REVEALS MOM AND MEGGIE ALSO DESCENDING PORCH STEPS
d3:33:11:25	1:58.75	CUT	CAMERA REVEALS BROTHER LOADING THE SUITCASE INTO THE JEEP
d3:33:13:02	1:59.99		CAMERA HOLDS AS RAIN WALKS TOWARD THE JEEP
d3:33:16:20	2:03.59		BROTHER GETS INTO JEEP
d3:33:17:19	2:04.58	CUT	MLS - MEGGIE AND JUSTINE
d3:33:19:11	2:06.29		THEY STAND AT THE BACK OF THE JEEP
d3:33:20:13	2:07.38		CAMERA FOLLOWS MEGGIE WALKING TOWARD THE JEEP
d3:33:23:08	2:10.20		SHE STANDS
d3:33:24:02	2:11.00		MEGGIE: **"WHERE'S RALPH?"**
d3:33:24:17	2:11.50		PAUSE
d3:33:28:18	2:13.53		AS RAIN STANDS: **"HE. . .ISN'T. . .RETURNING TO ROME. . ."**
d3:33:32:03	2:19.04	CUT	PAUSE IN MS - FAVORING MEGGIE, JUSTINE, AND FIONA STANDING ON THE PORCH
d3:33:33:13	2:20.37		RAIN: **"HE ASKS THAT WE GO ON WITHOUT HIM. . .HE'S VERY ILL MRS. O'NEILL"**
d3:33:37:12	2:24.34	CUT	PAUSE IN CS - RAIN
d3:33:39:01	2:25.98		RAIN: **"HE ASKED FOR YOU."**
d3:33:40:10	2:27.28	CUT	PAUSE IN MS - FAVORING MEGGIE, JUSTINE, AND FIONA STANDING ON THE PORCH
d3:33:41:10	2:28.28		MEGGIE SLIGHTLY NODS HER HEAD AFFIRMATIVE
d3:33:43:19	2:30.58		MEGGIE LOOKS TOWARD JUSTINE
d3:33:48:08	2:33.22		SHE WALKS TOWARD HER
d3:33:49:08	2:36.22		SHE STANDS IN FRONT OF JUSTINE

d3:33:50:24	2:37.76	CUT	CS - FAVORING MEGGIE
d3:33:53:20	2:40.88	CUT	CS - JUSTINE
d3:33:57:05	2:44.13	CUT	CS - MEGGIE
d3:34:00:12	2:47.03		THEY MOVE TOWARD EACH OTHER
d3:34:02:07	2:49.14	CUT	CS - JUSTINE
d3:34:03:28	2:50.84		SHE SMILES
d3:34:05:07	2:42.14	CUT	CS - MEGGIE SMILING
d3:34:10:29	2:57.88		MEGGIE GIVES JUSTINE A LITTLE KISS ON THE CHEEK
d3:34:11:14	2:58.38		THE TWO RELEASE THEIR EMBRACE
d3:34:19:24	3:06.72	CUT	PAUSE IN CS - JUSTINE
d3:34:20:11	3:07.29		SHE NODS HER HEAD AFFIRMATIVE
d3:34:21:06	3:08.12		MEGGIE GIVES HER A KISS ON THE CHEEK
d3:34:21:29	3:08.89		KISS ENDS
d3:34:22:08	3:09.18		JUSTINE LOOKS AT MEGGIE
d3:34:23:12	3:10.32	CUT	CS - FAVORING MEGGIE
d3:34:25:02	3:11.99		SHE SMILES AT HER
d3:34:25:17	3:12.49	CUT	MS - JUSTINE OVER MEGGIE'S SHOULDER
d3:34:27:01	3:13.98		THE TWO WALK TOWARD THE CAMERA AS CAMERA PULLS BACK
d3:34:31:02	3:18.00		RAIN HELPS JUSTINE INTO THE JEEP
d3:34:36:04	3:23.07		JUSTINE SITS AS RAIN TAKES MEGGIES' HANDS
d3:34:37:00	3:23.94		MEGGIE: **"THANK YOU."**
d3:34:37:22	3:24.67		PAUSE
d3:34:39:20	3:28.61		RAIN GETS INTO JEEP AS BROTHER STARTS THE MOTOR
d3:34:44:08	3:31.21		MEGGIE HOLDS HER HAND TOWARD JUSTINE AS THE JEEPS DRIVES OFF
d3:34:48:09	3:33.25		JEEP DRIVES OUT OF FRAME
d3:34:50:06	3:37.15	CUT	MS - JUSTINE WAVING GOODBYE
d3:34:50:21	3:37.65		SHE STOPS WAVING
d3:34:51:20	3:38.82		AND PUTS HER HAND ON RAIN'S
d3:34:57:07	3:44.19	CUT	FS - MEGGIE AND MOM STANDING ON THE PORCH
d3:35:02:12	3:49.30	CUT	CS - MEGGIE TURNING TOWARD CAMERA
d3:35:05:29	3:52.37	CUT	CS - MOM
d3:35:09:11	3:56.27	CUT	CS - MEGGIE SMILING AT MOM
d3:35:11:29	3:58.37		SHE LOOKS DOWN

Be Happy

:00
:02
:04
:06
:08
:10
:12
:14
Drogheda
Fl. a2
2 Flute
English Horn
2 Clarinet in B♭
Eng. Hn. & Cl. a3
3
3
Bassoon
3
3
3
Harp
Piano
mf
Ped.
Ped.
(Pno. muted)
Violin
div.
mp
Soli, unis.
mf
Viola
Violoncello
div.
mp
Contrabass
pizz.
mp

9
:16
:18
:20
:22
:24
:26
:28
Vln.
Va.
Vc.
Cb.

16
:30
:32
:34
:36
:38
:40
Ob.
Bsn.
3
mf
Vln.
div.
unis.
div
Va.
Vc.
Cb.

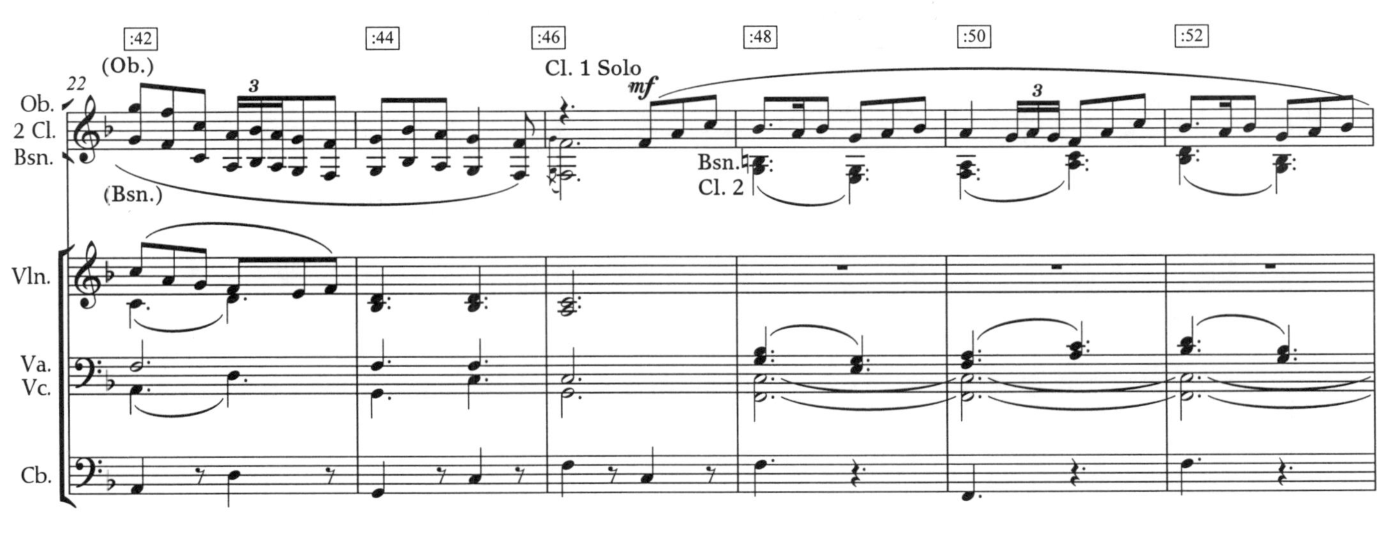

:42
:44
:46
:48
:50
:52
(Ob.)
3
Cl. 1 Solo
mf
3
Ob.
2 Cl.
Bsn.
(Bsn.)
Bsn.
Cl. 2
Vln.
Va.
Vc.
Cb.

:54
:56
:58
1:00
1:04
3
3
Cl.
Bsn.
12
8
Vln.
12
8
Va.
Vc.
12
8
Cb.
12
8

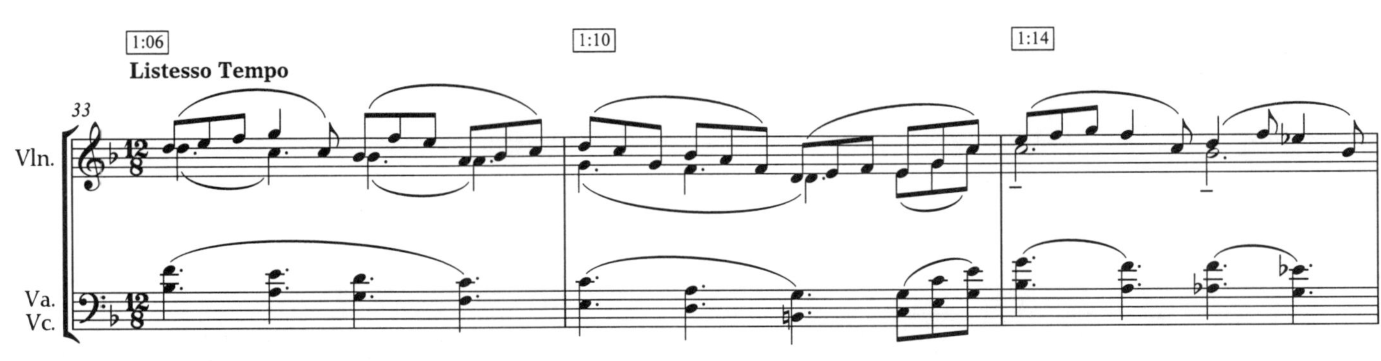

1:06
1:10
1:14
Listesso Tempo
33
Vln.
12
8
Va.
Vc.
12
8

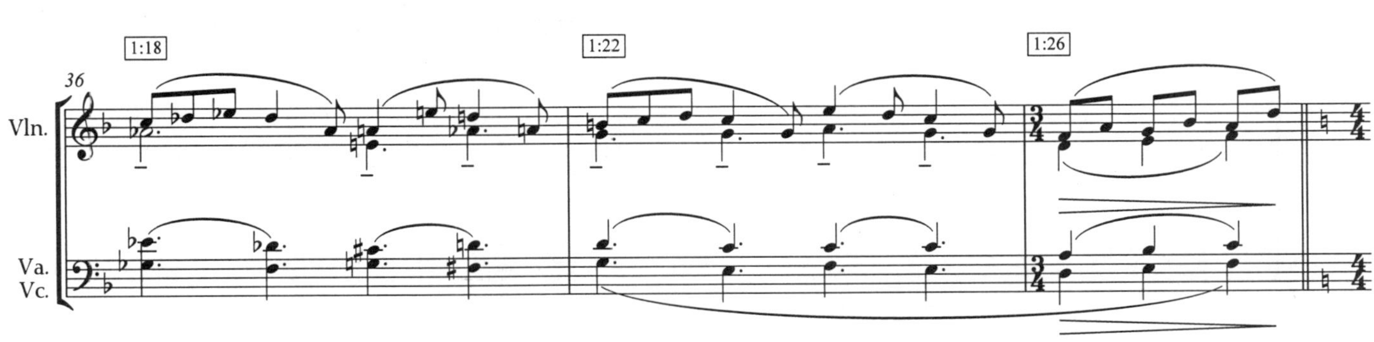

1:18
1:22
1:26
36
Vln.
3
4
4
4
Va.
Vc.
3
4
4
4

1:29.4
Shade faster
39
Solo
Fl.
mf
Shade faster
Vln.
p
Va.
Va.
Vc.
+ Vc.

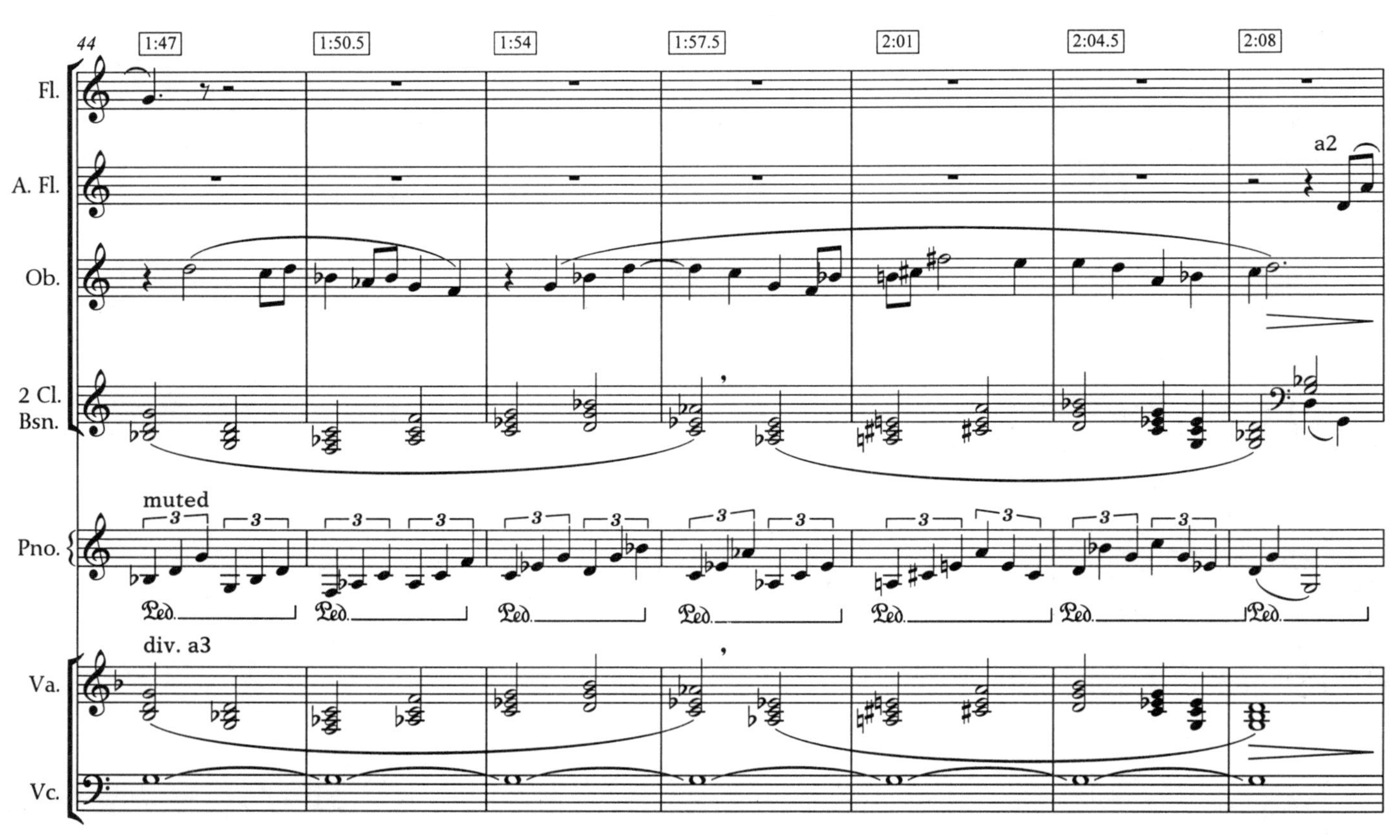

44
1:47
1:50.5
1:54
1:57.5
2:01
2:04.5
2:08
Fl.
A. Fl.
a2
Ob.
2 Cl.
Bsn.
muted
3 3 3 3 3 3 3 3 3 3 3 3 3 3
Pno.
Ped. Ped. Ped. Ped. Ped. Ped. Ped.
div. a3
Va.
Vc.

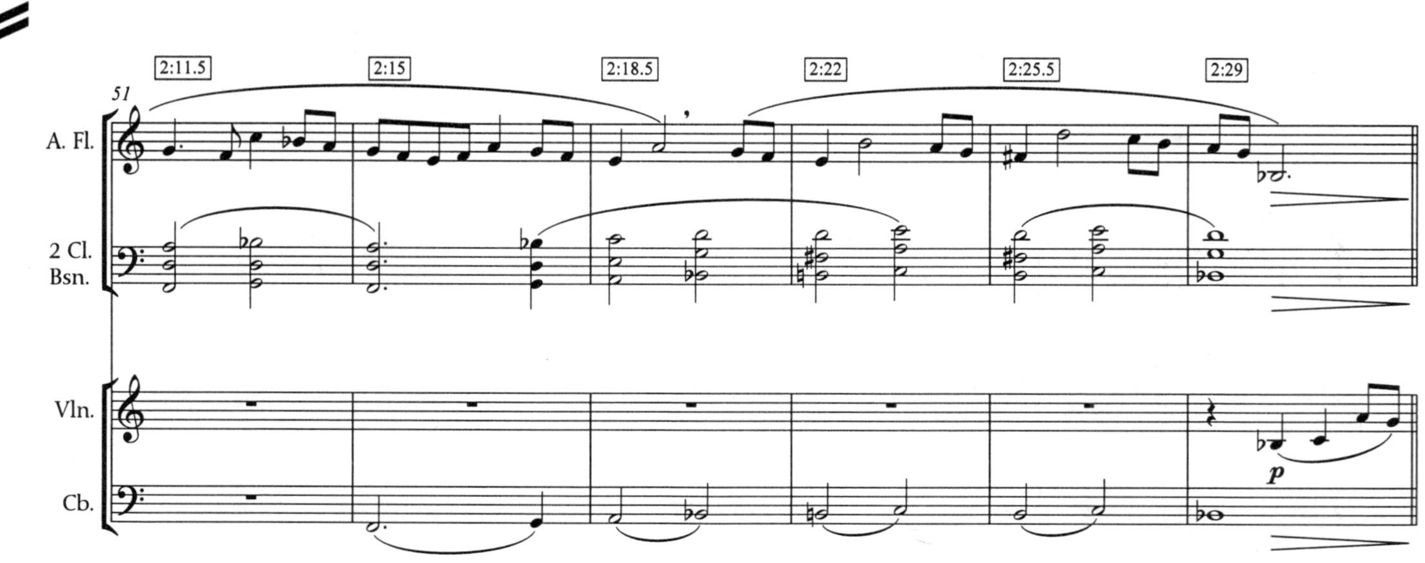

51
2:11.5
2:15
2:18.5
2:22
2:25.5
2:29
A. Fl.
2 Cl.
Bsn.
Vln.
p
Cb.

2:32.5
2:36
2:39.5
2:43
2:46.5
2:50
57
Walks to Justine
Vln.
Va.
Vc.
2:53.5
2:57
3:00.5
3:04
3:07.5
3:11
63
A. Fl.
Vln.
String quartet
pp
Va.
Vc.
3:14.5
3:18
3:21.5
3:25
3:28.5
3:32
69
A. Fl.
Eng. Hn.
Cl. 1
p
p
Cl. 2
Bsn.
p
Vln.
mf
Vc.
Va.
Vc.
mf
mf
Cb.
mf
3:35.5
3:39
3:42.5
3:46
3:49.5
75
Vln.
pp
pp
Va.
Vc.
Cb.
pp
pp

118

Cut to Fiona
Meggie walks to garden
Ralph in garden
muted
div. a3

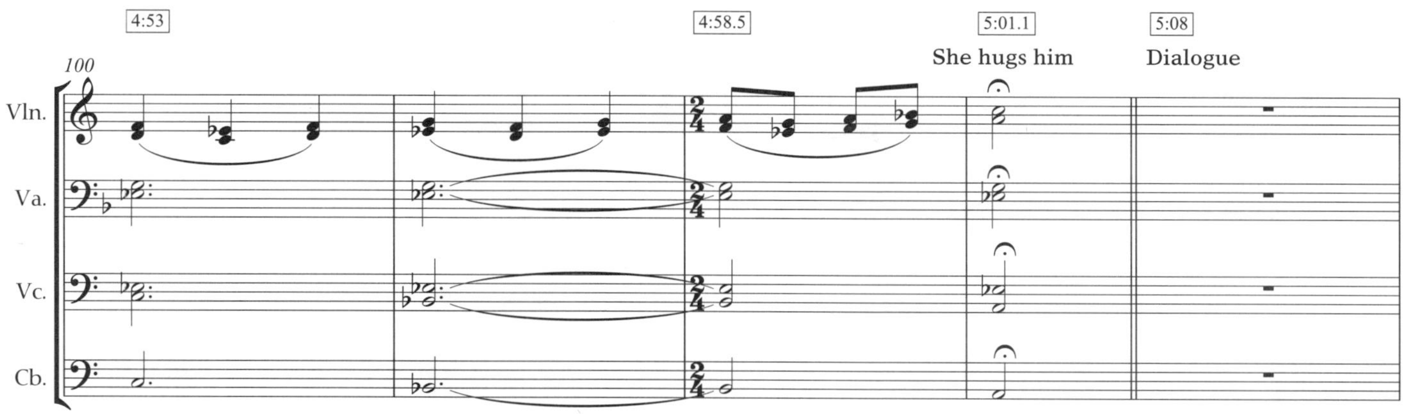

Example 16
M–28 The Final Scene (Episode IV)
⊙ CD Track 16

In the scene between M–27 and M–28, Ralph, now clearly near the end, finally sees all of the pain that he has caused Meggie and himself.

We start gently with just harp and muted piano. The low woodwinds doubled by the low strings form a soft, dark underscore to Ralph feeling a pain in his chest. He then recalls <u>The Story of the Thorn Bird.</u> We reprise the music, used in the first episode, at 32:4. The story ends. The low, soft unison violas lead to the celli and bass unison line that wends its way down finally resting on a low "A." This is allowed to fade away. As Ralph dies the (regular) piano, in octaves, reiterated the note in its lowest register, softly. The piano note is allowed to fade naturally at 2:03.6. We are in complete musical silence before Meggie, realizing that Ralph is dead, moves to their final embrace. At 2:24.3, we start our ascent to the final tutti, ending the film.

Production: **THE THORNBIRDS**   Production #: 167604
Cue: **M - 28 "THE FINAL SCENE"**
Begins at **d3:38:37:02**

ABS SMPTE #(df)	REL. TIME:	
		RALPH HAS BEEN TALKING WITH MEGGIE ABOUT HIS MISTAKES IN REGARD TO HER AND TO GOD.
d3:38:37:02	0:00.0	MUSIC BEGINS IN CS - HIS HAND ON HER HEAD
d3:38:37:10	0:00.27 CUT	CS - RALPH
d3:38:40:26	0:03.80	HE GIVES A SLIGHT INHALE OF PAIN
d3:38:42:05	0:05.11	HE BRINGS HIS HAND UP INTO VIEW HOLDING HIS CHEST
d3:38:44:29	0:07.91	WE SEE HE'S IN MORE PAIN
d3:38:46:11	0:09.31	HE CLOSES HIS EYES
d3:38:46:15	0:09.44	HE WINCES
d3:38:47:28	0:10.88	HE OPENS HIS EYES
d3:38:50:03	0:13.05 CUT	CS - HIS HAND ON HER HEAD
d3:38:52:18	0:15.55 CUT	MS - RALPH
d3:38:56:29	0:19.92	HE LOOKS DOWN AT MEGGIE

d3:38:57:15	0:20.45	CUT	CS - HIS HAND ON HER HEAD
d3:38:59:08	0:22.22		RALPH: **"LONG AGO. . ."**
d3:39:00:17	0:23.46	CUT	PAUSE IN MS - MEGGIE AND RALPH
d3:39:03:15	0:26.39		RALPH: **". . .I TOLD YOU A STORY. . .A LEGEND ABOUT A BIRD THAT SINGS ONLY WHEN IT DIES. . ."**
d3:39:09:01	0:31.93	CUT	PAUSE IN CS - MEGGIE SMILING
d3:39:12:13	0:35.34	CUT	MEGGIE: **"BIRD WITH A THORN IN IT'S BREAST. . .YOU SAID IT PAYS IT'S LIFE. . .THAT ONE SONG. . .BUT THE WHOLE WORLD STILLS TO LISTEN. . .AND GOD IN HEAVEN SMILES. . ."**
d3:39:30:16	0:53.45		PAUSE
d3:39:31:06	0:54.12	CUT	CS - RALPH
d3:39:31:16	0:54.52		RALPH: **"DRIVEN TO THE THORN WITH NO KNOWLEDGE OF THE DYING TO COME. . ."**
d3:39:36:05	0:59.09		PAUSE
d3:39:36:17	0:59.49	CUT	CS - HIS HAND ON HER HEAD
d3:39:37:11	1:00.29		SHE LIFTS HER HEAD
d3:39:38:11	1:01.29		SHE LOOKS AT HIM AS HE HOLDS HER FACE IN HIS HANDS
d3:39:40:12	1:03.33	CUT	CS - RALPH
d3:39:41:06	1:04.13		RALPH: **"BUT WHEN WE. . .WHEN WE PRESS THE THORN TO OUR BREAST. . .WE KNOW. . .WE UNDERSTAND. . ."**
d3:39:54:02	1:17.01	CUT	PAUSE IN CS - MEGGIE'S FACE
d3:39:56:17	1:19.51	CUT	CS - RALPH
d3:39:59:05	1:22.12		RALPH: **"AND STILL. . .WE DO IT. . ."**
d3:40:04:11	1:27.32		RALPH: **"STILL. . .WE DO IT. . ."**
d3:40:09:07	1:32.19	CUT	PAUSE IN CS - MEGGIE'S FACE
d3:40:11:12	1:34.36		SHE LOOKS TO HIS LEFT HAND
d3:40:13:17	1:36.53		SHE TAKES HIS HAND IN HERS
d3:40:15:16	1:38.50		RUBS HER CHEEK ON HIS HAND
d3:40:18:20	1:41.63		HE MOVES HIS HAND TO HER HEAD
d3:40:18:26	1:41.84	CUT	CS - RALPH
d3:40:21:25	1:44.80		HE LOOKS UP
d3:40:24:12	1:47.37		HE GASPS WITH PAIN
d3:40:26:18	1:49.58		HE LOOKS UP OFF STAGE
d3:40:32:11	1:55.35	CUT	CS - MEGGIE'S FACE IN RALPH'S LAP
d3:40:33:10	1:56.32		WE HEAR HIM GASP AGAIN
d3:40:34:09	1:57.28		HE RAISES HIS HAND OFF HER HEAD
d3:40:37:12	2:00.39		HE MOVES HIS HAND TOWARD THE CAMERA

d3:40:40:02	2:03.06		HIS HAND DROPS
d3:40:42:16	2:05.53		MEGGIE LOOKS UP
d3:40:43:12	2:06.39		SHE LOOKS AT HIS HAND
d3:40:44:06	2:07.19		SHE LOOKS UP AT RALPH
d3:40:45:10	2:08.33	CUT	CS - RALPH'S HEAD RESTING ON HIS CHEST
d3:40:47:24	2:10.80	CUT	CS - MEGGIE LOOKING UP AT HIM
d3:40:49:21	2:12.70		SHE MOVES HER HAND TOWARD HIM
d3:40:52:10	2:15.34	CUT	CS - RALPH AS MEGGIE TOUCHES HER CHEEK
d3:40:59:11	2:22.38	CUT	CS - MEGGIE MOVING UP TOWARD HIM
d3:41:00:20	2:23.61		SHE WRAPS HER ARMS AROUND HIM
d3:41:20:02	2:43.03	CUT	CS - RALPH AND MEGGIE
d3:41:25:12	2:48.37		SHE SLOWLY MOVES AWAY FROM HIM
d3:41:27:22	2:50.70		SHE SLOWLY SLIDES HER HANDS AWAY FROM HIS FACE
d3:41:31:12	2:54.37		HER HANDS ARE FULLY AWAY FROM HIS FACE
d3:41:33:23	2:56.74	CUT	CS - FAVORING MEGGIE LOOKING AT RALPH
d3:41:35:05	2:58.14		SHE LOOKS AWAY FROM HIM. . .
d3:41:37:04	3:00.11		RESTING HER HAND ON HIS HANDS
d3:41:39:27	3:02.88	CUT	FS - SHEEP AND PLANE TAKING OFF TOWARD THE CAMERA
d3:41:45:04	3:08.12		PLANE IS AIRBORNE
d3:41:50:24	3:13.79		CAMERA PANS RIGHT FOLLOWING PLANE
d3:41:52:16	3:15.53		PLANE FLIES IN FRONT OF CAMERA
d3:42:09:01	3:31.98	CUT	MS - MEGGIE AND RALPH
d3:42:12:24	3:35.75		PLANE FLIES TOWARD CAMERA
d3:42:15:28	3:38.89		CAMERA PANS RIGHT FOLLOWING PLANE
d3:42:21:17	3:44.52		CAMERA HOLD IN FS - ROSE GARDEN
d3:42:22:03	3:45.06		PLANE FLIES OUT OF VIEW
d3:42:37:00	3:59.97		START FADE OUT
d3:42:38:03	4:01.07		MUSIC FULL OUT TO BLACK AND END OF SHOW
			TOTAL TIME - 4:01.07

The Final Scene

1:04
1:07
1:10
1:13
1:16
1:19
19
Solo
A. Fl.
Pno.
Ped. Ped. Ped. Ped. Ped. Ped.
Vln.
1:22
1:25
1:28
1:32
1:35
1:38
1:41
25
(A. Fl. Solo)
+ A. Fl. 2 & Bsn.
2 A. Fl.
Bsn.
Vln.
Va.
Vc.
Cb.
1:44
1:48
1:52
2:00
2:03.6
32
He stiffens with pain
Ralph dies
Pno.
(Vc.)
Va.
Vc.
8vb
Cb.
2:24.3
2:26.5
2:29
2:31.5
2:34
2:36.5
38
Faster
Hn.
Tbn.
Tba.
Hp.
Pno.
unis.
Vln.
Va.
mf
Vc.
Cb.

Fl., Ob. a3
Cl., Bsn. a3
2 Fl.
Ob.
2 Cl.
Bsn.
Hn.
Tbn.
Tba.
Hp.
Pno.
Vln.
Va.
Vc.
Cb.
a3
mf
mf
44
2:39
2:41.5
2:44
2:46.5
2:49
49 (a3)
2:51.5
2:54
2:56.5
2:59
3:01.5

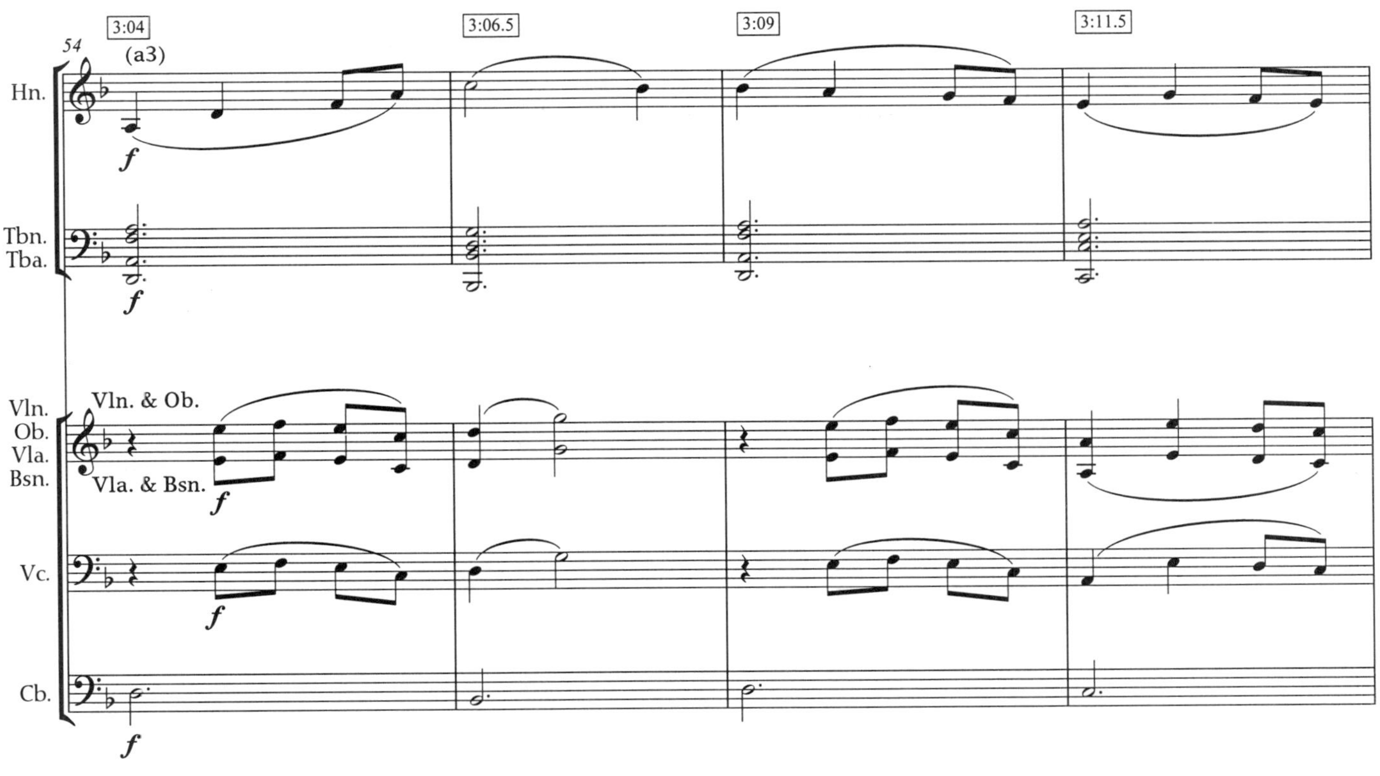
3:04
3:06.5
3:09
3:11.5
54
Hn.
(a3)
f
Tbn.
Tba.
f
Vln.
Ob.
Vla.
Bsn.
Vln. & Ob.
Vla. & Bsn.
f
Vc.
f
Cb.
f

3:14
3:16.5
3:19
3:21.5
58
2 Fl.
2 Cl.
f cresc.
Hn.
(a3)
Tbn.
Tba.
Vln.
Ob.
Vla.
Bsn.
Vc.
Cb.

3:24
3:26.5
3:29
3:31.5
3:34
2 Fl.
2 Cl.
2 Ob.
Bsn.
3 Tpt.
a3
mf
Hn.
(a3)
Tbn.
Tba.
Hp.
Pno.
mp
Ped.
Vln.
Va.
Vc.
Cb.
62

3:36.5
3:39
3:41.5
3:44
67
2 Fl.
2 Ob.
2 Cl.
Fl. &
Ob., a4
Cl. a2
Bsn.
3 Tpt.
(a3)
Hn.
(a3)
Tbn.
Tba.
Hp.
Pno.
Ped.
Ped.
Ped.
Ped.
Vln.
Va.
Vc.
Cb.
Timp.

3:50
3:52.5
3:55
4:01.5
71
2 Fl.
2 Ob.
2 Cl.
Bsn.
3 Tpt.
Hn.
Tbn.
Tba.
(Hp.)
Hp.
Pno.
ad. Lib.
Vln.
Va.
Vc.
Cb.
Timp.
sffz

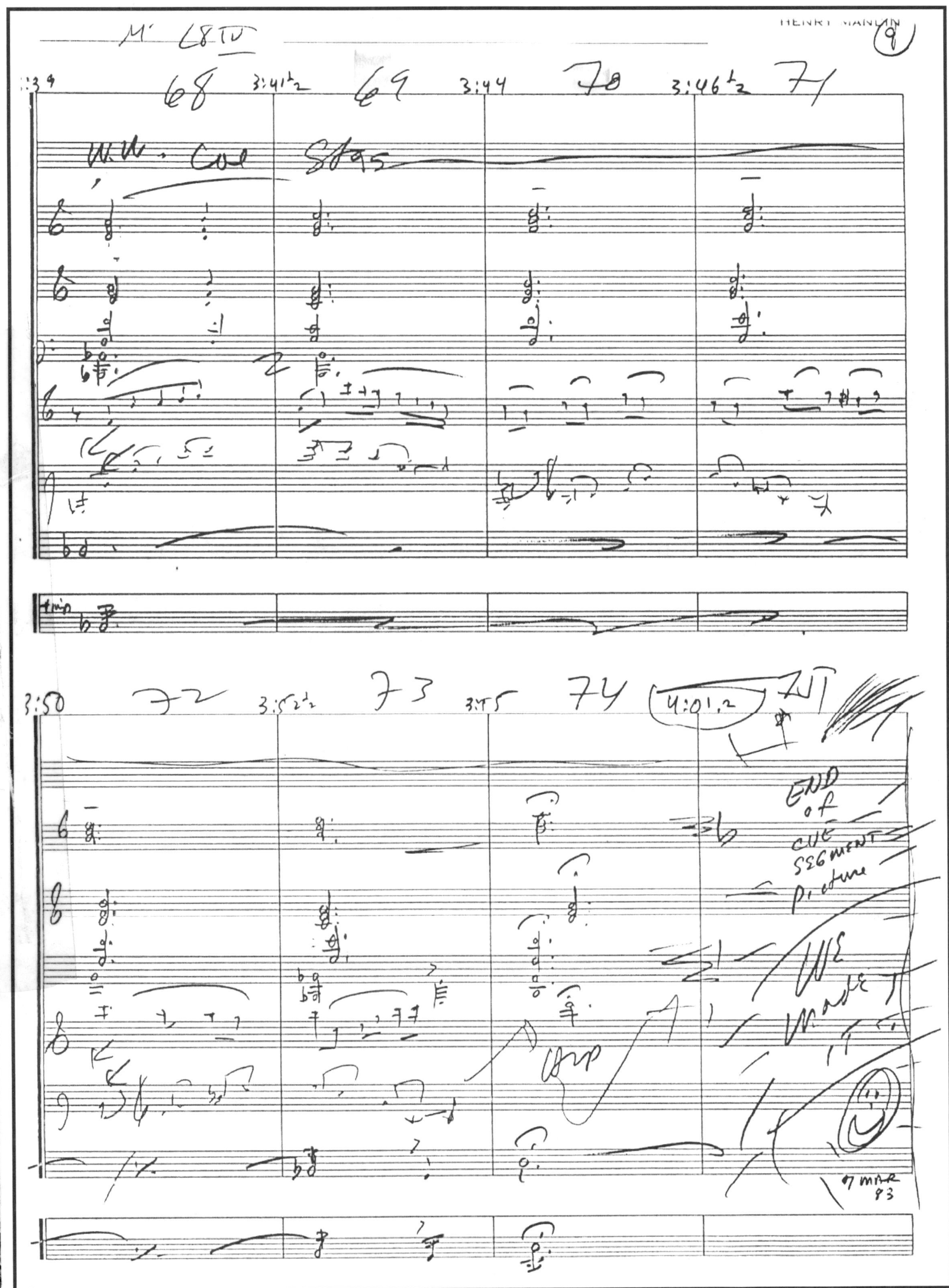
M. L8 IV
HENRY MANCINI
9
1:39
68   3:41½   69   3:44   70   3:46½   71
W.W. Cue Stops
4 min
3:50   72   3:52½   73   3:55   74   4:01.2   RIT
END
of
CUE
SEGMENT
picture
WE
MADE
IT
7 MAR
83

Last Words

I feel that the old adage of "a good score is one that you're not aware of" is only half true. Granted, under dialogue, a low profile must be kept. However, if the viewer in unaware of the music during a three minute Main Title, the composer isn't saying much.

With new technology entering the media at a blinding pace, we are constantly being put into new learning situations. Acknowledging that and realizing that one must keep up, I maintain that the real creative power is in the mind and heart of the composer. I have never seen nor heard of a computer that could make you cry.

Music can.

☙❧